The Application of the High Seas Regime in the Exclusive Economic Zone

Frank-Luke Attard Camilleri

Hamilton Books

Lanham • Boulder • New York • Toronto • Plymouth, UK

4501 Forbes Boulevard, Suite 200, Lanham, Maryland 20706
Hamilton Books Acquisitions Department (301) 459-3366

Unit A, Whitacre Mews, 26-34 Stannary Street,
London SE11 4AB, United Kingdom

Printed in the United States of America
British Library Cataloguing in Publication Information Available

Library of Congress Control Number: 2017942134
ISBN: 978-0-7618-6950-4 (cloth : alk. paper)—ISBN: 978-0-7618-6951-1 (electronic)

∞™ The paper used in this publication meets the minimum requirements of American National Standard for Information Sciences Permanence of Paper for Printed Library Materials, ANSI/NISO Z39.48-1992.

To the People of Malta for investing in me

To my parents and loved ones *ab imo pectore*

For all lovers of the sea

Contents

Table of Legal Instruments

1844 Convention for the Protection of Submarine Telegraph Cables (adopted 14 March 1884, entered into force 1 May 1888) TS 380

1921 Barcelona Convention and Statue on Freedom of Transit (adopted 20 April 1921, entered 31 October 1922)

1944 Convention on International Civil Aviation (adopted 7 December 1944, entered into force 4 April 1947) 15 UNTS 295

1947 General Agreement on Tariffs and Trade (adopted 30 October 1947, entered into force 1 January 1948) 55 UNTS 194

1958 Convention on the Continental Shelf (adopted 29 April 1958, entered into force 10 June 1964) 499 UNTS 311

1958 Convention on the High Seas (adopted 29 April 1958, entered into force 30 September 1962) 450 UNTS 11

1965 Convention on Transit Trade of Land-Locked States (adopted 8 July 1965, entered 9 June 1967) 597 UNTS 3

1972 Convention on the International Regulations for Prevention Collisions at Sea (adopted 20 October 1972, entered into force 15 July 1977) 1050 UNTS 16

1982 United Nations Convention on the Law of the Sea (10 December 1982, entered into force 16 November 1994) 1833 UNTS 3

1996 Protocol to the Convention on the Prevention of Marine Pollution by Dumping of Wastes and Other Matter of 29 December 1972 (adopted 7 November 1996, entered into force 24 March 2006) 2006 ATS 11

2001 UNESCO Convention on the Protection of the Underwater Cultural Heritage (adopted 2 November 2001, entered into force 2 January 2009) 2562 UNTS 1

Table of Judgments

Anglo-Norwegian Fisheries Case (United Kingdom v Norway) (Merits) [1951] ICJ Rep 3

Continental Shelf Case (Libyan Arab Jamahiriya v Malta) (Merits) [1985] ICJ Rep 3

Gulf of Maine Case (Canada v United States) (Merits) [1984] ICJ Rep 165

Lotus Case (France v Turkey) (Merits) [1927] PCIJ Rep Series A No 10

Nicaragua Case (Nicaragua v United States of America) (Merits) [1986] ICJ Rep 14

North Sea Continental Shelf Cases (Federal Republic of Germany v Denmark; Federal Republic of Germany v Netherlands) (Merits) [1969] ICJ Rep 3

Nuclear Tests Case (Australia v France) (Merits) [1974] ICJ Rep 253

Nuclear Tests Case (New Zealand v France) (Merits) [1974] ICJ Rep 457

Acknowledgments

I owe my gratitude to a great many people who have made this book possible and because of whom my postgraduate experience has been one that I will truly cherish forever.

My deepest gratitude is to my supervisor, Professor Patricia Vella de Fremeaux and to my co-supervisor, Dr Felicity Attard. I am very thankful for their professional supervision, guidance and advice.

I am also deeply grateful to the numerous academic and administrative personnel from the Universities of Yale, Oxford and Virginia for their collaboration and invaluable help at different stages of my research.

I am also indebted to the staff of the University of Malta Library for their continuous assistance. I would also like to acknowledge the assistance of Ms Verica Cole, Librarian at the IMO International Maritime Law Institute and other staff at the IMO International Maritime Law Institute.

I am also thankful to Professor Kevin Aquilina and the staff at the University of Malta – Faculty of Laws for their support and dedication.

I would also like to acknowledge the encouragement and practical advice offered by various foreign lawyers and diplomats, particularly British, Australian and American, whose friendship I greatly value. I owe my deep appreciation to many friends, local and foreign, who were behind me throughout this challenging period.

Finally, I would like to express my heartfelt gratitude to my immediate and extended family, for their endless love, concern and support without which this would not have been possible.

Multas gratias vobis ago.

Abbreviations

ADIZ: Air Defence Identification Zone
EEZ: Exclusive Economic Zone
HSC: Geneva Convention on the High Seas, 1958
ICAO: International Civil Aviation Organisation
ICPC: International Cable Protection Committee
IMLI: International Maritime Law Institute
IMO: International Maritime Organisation
NATO: North Atlantic Treaty Organisation
OPAC: Online Public Access Catalogue
UNESCO: United Nations Educational, Scientific and Cultural Organisation
UNCLOS: United Nations Convention on the Law of the Sea
UNCLOS I: First United Nations Conference on the Law of the Sea
UNCLOS II: Second United Nations Conference on the Law of the Sea
UNCLOS III: Third United Nations Conference on the Law of the Sea

Introduction

To What Extent Is the High Seas Regime Applicable in the EEZ?

CONTEXT AND OBJECTIVES[1]

The world's oceans cover more than seventy percent of the Earth's surface,[2] where the vast majority of ocean space consists of areas beyond the national jurisdiction of any State, known as high seas.[3]

The high seas regime is one of the oldest institutions of the law of the sea, dating back to Grotius' *Mare Liberum* published in 1613.[4] A significant step forward in the development of the high seas regime was the adoption of the 1958 Geneva Convention on the High Seas,[5] at the First United Nations Conference on the Law of the Sea (UNCLOS I). This Convention was significant as it codified the rules of customary international law relating to the high seas such as non-appropriation of the high seas,[6] freedom of navigation[7] and flag State exclusivity.[8] The high seas were traditionally defined as 'all parts of the sea not included in the territorial sea or in the internal waters of a state'.[9] This definition was then modified due to the advent of the concepts of the Exclusive Economic Zone (EEZ) and archipelagic waters under the law of the sea.[10]

The high seas regime was then further elaborated upon in Part VII[11] of the United Nations Convention on the Law of the Sea (UNCLOS),[12] adopted at the Third United Nations Conference on the Law of the Sea (UNCLOS III). This part sets out legal rules governing the use of the high seas. Article 86[13] states that the high seas rules in the Convention apply to:

> all parts of the seas that are not included in the exclusive economic zone, in the territorial sea or in the internal waters of a State, or in the archipelagic waters of an archipelagic State.[14]

The high seas are governed by certain fundamental principles.[15] In particular, the high seas are open to all States, whether coastal or land-locked.[16] No State may validly purport to subject any part of them to its sovereignty.[17] From this it follows that States are free to use the high seas for any lawful purpose and as a rule it is only the flag State which has jurisdiction over its registered vessels on the high seas.[18]

On the high seas, all States are free to exercise certain freedoms, however, these are subject to certain requirements under UNCLOS including the 'due regard'[19] principle and other general rules of international law,[20] like the rules governing the use of force.

Whilst the high seas regime is one of the oldest institutions of the law of the sea,[21] the EEZ is 'a significant innovation of UNCLOS'.[22] As Robertson writes 'the most significant outcome of UNCLOS III was the recognition in the Convention at that Conference of the exclusive economic zone (EEZ).'[23]

The Informal Single Negotiating Text of 1975 gave no formal definition of the EEZ but elaborated on the concept by specifying the rights and jurisdictions of the coastal State.[24] Today Article 55[25] defines the EEZ as:

> an area beyond and adjacent to the territorial sea, subject to the specific legal regime established in this Part, under which the rights and jurisdiction of the coastal State and the rights and freedoms of other States are governed by the relevant provisions of this Convention.[26]

The legal status of the EEZ was extensively dealt with during the early stages of UNCLOS III. As Churchill and Lowe[27] put it many maritime States[28] argue that the EEZ should have a residual high seas character. However, Articles 55[29] and 86[30] make it clear that the EEZ does not have a residual high seas character. Article 55[31] provides that the EEZ is 'subject to the specific legal regime established in this [EEZ] Part'[32] whilst Article 86[33] states that 'this [high seas] Part apply to all parts of the sea that are not included in the exclusive economic zone…'.[34] Still, the EEZ may not be acquainted with a residual territorial sea character. Beckman and Davenport argue that Article 55[35] makes it clear that the EEZ is a regime that is neither under the sovereignty of the coastal State nor part of the high seas, but a special, *sui generis* regime.[36] The opinions of the authors[37] have remained divided on this issue.

It can be argued that the EEZ has a *sui generis* legal status and as Castañeda writes 'does not form part of the territorial sea nor of the high seas'.[38] Churchill and Lowe[39] specify the three principal elements of the *sui generis* legal character of the EEZ of which the 'rights and duties which the

Law of the Sea Convention accords to the coastal State[40] and the 'rights and duties which the Convention accords to other States'[41] are core to this book and will in fact be considered at a later stage.

Although within the EEZ, a coastal State has sovereign rights, certain high seas freedoms apply in the water column despite it is not high seas. This book will therefore aim to examine to what extent is the high seas regime applicable in the EEZ.

According to Oxman,[42] supporters of the theory that the EEZ has a high seas character argue that the result of Articles 58[43] and 86[44] of the Convention is that the sea is not divided geographically between the EEZ and the high seas, but that there is a functional relationship in which each of these provisions applies the same norms. From this perspective the freedoms and uses would be the same in either case. However, as Orrega Vicuña writes, when looking at the problem from the thesis of the EEZ as a *sui generis* institution, the situation is different. The fact that some aspects of the EEZ are related to the freedoms of the high seas does not mean that the two regimes intermix.[45] According to what Article 86[46] states each regime maintains its own sphere of application.

The relationship between the EEZ and the high seas is interesting and worth further exploring because it defines the character of the EEZ itself; it outlines which parts of the high seas regime are applicable in the EEZ and highlights the rights of both coastal States and other States in the EEZ. This book seeks to examine this relationship between the EEZ and the high seas regime. More precisely the author intends to examine the applicability of the high seas regime in the EEZ so as to demonstrate the importance of the EEZ and throw more light on how the sovereign rights of States in the EEZ may limit the freedoms of the high seas in the EEZ.

This book seeks to examine Articles 86 and 87 in the light of UNCLOS Article 58. Article 58[47] specifies the rights and duties of other States in the EEZ. It explicitly states that 'articles 88 to 115 and other pertinent rules of international law apply to the exclusive economic zone in so far as they are not incompatible with this Part'.[48] These three Articles are key to when analysing the application of the high seas regime in the EEZ. Articles 86[49] and 87[50] in essence relate to the high seas regime whereas UNCLOS Article 58 is, as explained, about the position in the EEZ. Article 58[51] is about the rights and duties of other States in the EEZ. Analysing the relationship between these three articles is crucial to draw the relationship between the EEZ and the high seas regime, as these three articles are major in this area of research.

It results from Article 58[52] that only three freedoms of the high seas i.e. (i) the freedom of navigation; (ii) the freedom of overflight and (iii) the freedom to lay submarine cables and pipelines are open to all States in the EEZ. Yet these three freedoms suffer greater limitations than on the high seas mainly because, as explained above, in the EEZ we have to consider the sovereign rights of the different coastal States.

Some of the main research questions this book seeks to address include; to what extent is the high seas freedom of navigation applicable in the EEZ? To what extent is the high seas freedom of overflight applicable in the EEZ? And to what extent is the high seas freedom to lay submarine cables and pipelines applicable in the EEZ?

This book is to devote a chapter to each of the three freedoms highlighted above so as to carefully examine how each high seas freedom is limited in an EEZ context.

Chapter one will examine the freedom of navigation on the high seas and study its application in the EEZ.

Chapter two is concerned with the high seas freedom of overflight and its application in the EEZ. Chapter three focuses on the high seas freedom to lay submarine cables and pipelines and its relevance in an EEZ context. The conclusions aim to sum up on the main ideas of this book.

METHODOLOGY AND SOURCES

This book aims to mainly focus on documentary materials including major international law instruments such as the 1958 HSC, UNCLOS, as well as the Virginia Commentary on UNCLOS,[53] journal articles, books, reports amongst others.

This research is being conducted through the University of Malta and the International Maritime Organisation (IMO) International Maritime Law Institute (IMLI) libraries, using a range of information sources such as the Online Public Access Catalogue (OPAC) system, internet search engines, bibliographic databases and academic abstracts. The present holdings of the IMLI library in particular 'include most of the major textbooks in the field of international maritime law'.[54] The author will also obtain valuable material via academics from foreign universities including Yale University and the Universities of Oxford and Virginia so as to critically examine the existing research that is significant to this study. This book seeks to evaluate what has already been examined in this area and how the research can contribute further to the subject.

LIMITATIONS

The high seas and the EEZ are two very extensive areas about which a lot could be written. The author is to strictly limit this book to the application of the high seas regime in the EEZ so as to comprehensively answer the main question and its related sub-questions.

When conducting extensive research in this area of the law of the sea, certain difficulties may arise. The main hurdle is the limited period of this research and the amount of technical material required to focus on the complex relationship that exists between the high seas and the EEZ.

NOTES

1. See in general on the law of the sea Myres Smith McDougal and William Thomas Burke, *The Public Order of the Oceans: A Contemporary International Law of the Sea* (Martinus Nijhoff Publishers, 1987); Nguyen Quoc Dinh, Patrick Daillier and Alain Pellet, *Droit International Public* (LGDJ 2002); Martine Rémond-Gouilloud, *Droit Maritime* (Editions A. Pedone, 1993); Constantine John Colombos, *The International Law of the Sea* (Longmans, 1967); Edward Duncan Brown, *The International Law of the Sea* (Dartmouth, 1994); Sir Robert Jennings and Sir Arthur Watts, *Oppenheim's International Law* (Oxford University Press, 2008); Philip Allott, "Mare Nostrum: A New International Law of the Sea" *American Journal of International Law* 86 (1992) 764-787; Réne Jean Dupuy and Daniel Vignes, *Traité du Nouveau Droit de la Mer* (Economica, 1985); Daniel Patrick O'Connell, *The International Law of the Sea* (Oxford University Press, 1982-1984); Shigeru Oda, *The Law of the Sea in Our Time* (Sijthoff, 1977); Tullio Treves, "Codification du Droit International et Pratique des Etats dans le Droit de le Mer" *Collected Courses of the Hague Academy of International Law* 223 (1990) 9-217; Daniel Bardonnet, Michael Virally and Guy de Lacharrière, *Le Nouveau Droit International de la Mer* (Editions A. Pedone, 1983); Derek Bowett, *Law of the Sea* (Manchester University Press, 1967); Gerard J. Mangone, *Law for the World Ocean* (Eastern Law House, 1981); Herbert A. Smith, *The Law and Custom of the Sea* (Stevens and Sons Limited, 1959); Ram Prakash Anand, *Origin and Development of the Law of the Sea* (Martinus Nijhoff Publishers, 1982); Oliver de Ferron, *Le droit international de la mer* (Librairie Minard, 1958) and Gilbert Gidel, *Le droit international public de la mer* (Mellottee, 1932-1934).

2. See http://www.noaa.gov/ocean.html accessed 27 November 2015.

3. Marjo Vierros, Anne McDonald, and Salvatore Arico, "Governance of marine areas beyond national jurisdictions" [2012] UNU Rio+20 Series 1, 1-2.

4. Hugo Grotius, *The Freedom of the Seas: or, The Right which Belongs to the Dutch to Take Part in the East Indian Trade*, trans. Ralph Magoffin (Oxford University Press, 1916); see also Tullio Treves, "Historical Development of the Law of the Sea" in Donald Rothwell, Alex Oude Elferink, Karen Scott and Tim Stephens, *The Oxford Handbook of the Law of the Sea* (Oxford University Press, 2015) 1-6.

5. Convention on the High Seas (adopted 29 April 1958, entered into force 30 September 1962) 450 UNTS 11, hereinafter referred to as 1958 HSC.

6. 1958 HSC, Article 2. This principle is now also codified in the United Nations Convention on the Law of the Sea (10 December 1982, entered into force 16 November 1994) 1833 UNTS 3, Part VII, Article 87, hereinafter referred to as UNCLOS. 'The non-appropriation principle is closely linked to the freedoms of the high seas, with article 89 being interpreted as the counterpart to this principle'; see David Joseph Attard and Patricia Mallia, "The High Seas" in David Joseph Attard, Malgosia Fitzmaurice and Norman A. Martínez Gutiérrez, *The IMLI Manual on International Maritime Law* (Oxford University Press, 2014) 242-243.

7. As Dupuy and Vignes explain in *A Handbook on the New Law of the Sea*, freedom of navigation is a principle of customary international law that, apart from the exceptions provided for in international law, ships flying the flag of any sovereign State shall not suffer interference from any other State. It was codified in the 1958 HSC, Article 2. This principle is now also codified in the UNCLOS, Part VII, Article 87; see Réne Jean Dupuy and Daniel Vignes, *A Handbook on the New Law of the Sea: Volume 1* (Martinus Nijhoff Publishers, 1991) 383-392.

8. 1958 HSC, Articles 5 and 6. This principle is now also codified in the UNCLOS, Part VII, Articles 92 and 94.

9. 1958 HSC, Article 1.

10. Robin Churchill and Alan Vaughn Lowe, *The Law of the Sea* (Manchester University Press, 1988) 164-176; see in general on the EEZ Benedetto Conforti, *Zona Economica Esclusiva* (Giuffrè, 1983); see also Winston Conrad Extavour, *The Exclusive Economic Zone: A Study of the Evolution and Progressive Development of the International Law of the Sea* (Sijthoff, 1979); see also Ann L. Hollick, "The Origins of 200 Mile Offshore Zones" *American Journal of International Law* 71 (1977) 494-500; see also Jonathan I. Charney, "The Exclusive Economic Zone and Public International Law" *Ocean Development and International Law* 15 (1985) 233-288; see also Robin Churchill and Alan Vaughn Lowe (n 10) 133-152.

11. UNCLOS, Part VII, Sections 1-2, Articles 86-120; see in general on UNCLOS Robin Churchill, "The 1982 United Nations Convention on the Law of the Sea" in Donald Rothwell, Alex Oude Elferink, Karen Scott and Tim Stephens, *The Oxford Handbook of the Law of the Sea* (Oxford University Press, 2015) 24-29.

12. Ibid.

13. Ibid, Article 86.

14. Ibid; see on the territorial sea Percy Thomas Flenn, "Origins of the Theory of Territorial Waters" *American Journal of International Law* 20 (1926) 465-482; see also Antonio Cassese, *International Law* (Oxford University Press, 2005) 84-91; see also James Crawford, *Brownlie's Principles of Public International Law* (Oxford University Press, 2012) 255-280; see on the internal waters V. D. Degan, "Internal Waters" *Netherlands Yearbook of International Law* 17 (1986) 3-44; see on archipelagic waters Dale Andrew, "Archipelagos and the Law of the Sea" Marine Policy 2 (1978) 45-64; see also Renaud Lattion, *L'Archipel en Droit International* (Editions Payot, 1984).

15. See on the high seas Douglas Guilfoyle, "The High Seas" in Donald Rothwell, Alex Oude Elferink, Karen Scott and Tim Stephens, *The Oxford Handbook of the Law of the Sea* (Oxford University Press, 2015) 203-212; see also Nguyen Quoc Dinh, Patrick Daillier and Alain Pellet (n 1) 1194; see also Sir Robert Jennings and Sir Arthur Watts (n 1) 710.

16. UNCLOS, Part VII, Section 1, Article 87.

17. Robin Churchill and Alan Vaughn Lowe (n 10) 164–176.

18. UNCLOS, Part VII, Section 1, Article 92.

19. Ibid, Article 87.

20. Ibid.

21. Hugo Grotius (n 4).

22. Robert Beckman, and Tara Davenport, "The EEZ Regime: Reflections after 30 Years" [2012] LOSI Conference Papers 1, 2.

23. Horace B. Robertson, "Navigation in the Exclusive Economic Zone" *Virginia Journal of International Law* 24 (1984) 865-866; see in general on the EEZ Gemma Andreone, "The Exclusive Economic Zone" in Donald Rothwell, Alex Oude Elferink, Karen Scott and Tim Stephens, *The Oxford Handbook of the Law of the Sea* (Oxford University Press, 2015) 159-178.

24. Francisco Orrego Vicuña, *The Exclusive Economic Zone, Regime and Legal Nature under International Law* (Cambridge University Press, 1989) 16 – 48.

25. UNCLOS, Part V, Article 55.

26. Ibid.

27. Robin Churchill and Alan Vaughn Lowe (n 10) 133 – 152.

28. The traditional naval powers including for example the former Soviet Union.

29. UNCLOS, Part V, Article 55.

30. Ibid, Part VII, Section 1, Article 86.

31. Ibid, Part V, Article 55.

32. Ibid.

33. Ibid, Part VII, Section 1, Article 86.

34. Ibid.

35. Ibid, Part V, Article 55.

36. Robert Beckman and Tara Davenport (n 22) 2.

37. Many different authors including for example Jorge Castañeda, Mario Scerni, Bernard H. Oxman, and Shigeru Oda. See Jorge Castañeda, "Negotiations on the Exclusive Economic Zone at the Third United Nations Conference on the Law of the Sea" in Jerzy Makarczyk,

Essays in International Law in Honour of Judge Manfred Lachs (Martinus Nijhoff Publishers, 1984) 621; see also Mario Scerni, "La Zone Économique Exclusive: Son Importance, sa Nature Juridique et les Problèmes Principaux Relatifs" in *Thesaurus Acroasium of the Institute of Public International Law and International Relations of Thessaloniki: Volume VII* (Thessaloniki Institute of Public International Law and International Relations, 1977) 183; see also Bernard H. Oxman, "An Analysis of the Exclusive Economic Zone as formulated in the Informal Composite Negotiating Text" in Thomas A. Clingan, *Law of the Sea: State Practice in Zones of Special Jurisdiction* (Honolulu Law of the Sea Institute, 1982) 77; see also Shigeru Oda, *International Law of the Resources of the Sea* (Sijthoff & Noordhoff, 1979) 37.

38. Jorge Castañeda (n 37) 621.
39. Robin Churchill and Alan Vaughn Lowe (n 10) 133 – 152.
40. Ibid.
41. Ibid.
42. Bernard H. Oxman (n 37) 69, 76-77.
43. UNCLOS, Part V, Article 58.
44. Ibid. Part VII, Section 1, Article 86.
45. Francisco Orrega Vicuña (n 24), 16 – 48.
46. UNCLOS, Part VII, Section 1, Article 86.
47. Ibid, Article 58.
48. Ibid.
49. Ibid, Article 86.
50. Ibid, Article 87.
51. Ibid, Article 58.
52. Ibid.
53. John Norton Moore, Myron H. Nordquist, Satya N. Nandan and Shabtai Rosenne, *United Nations Convention on the Law of the Sea 1982: A Commentary* (Martinus Nijhoff Publishers, 1993).
54. See http://www.imli.org/about-us/imli-library accessed 02 November 2015.

Chapter One

The Freedom of Navigation in the EEZ

1.1 INTRODUCTION

The freedom of navigation is one of the oldest and most recognized principles in the legal regime governing ocean space.[1] It may be argued that since it was enshrined in the 1609 treatise[2] of Hugo Grotius this principle may constitute one of the pillars of the law of the sea and was at the origins of modern international law.[3]

UNCLOS makes ample reference to the freedom of navigation for example in Articles 17 to 26,[4] 36,[5] 38,[6] 52,[7] 58,[8] 78[9] and 87.[10] All these articles refer to the freedom of navigation which basically means freedom of movement of vessels. What distinguishes the freedom of navigation in the different zones of the sea is the different influence coastal States may exercise on the freedom of movement.[11]

1.2 NAVIGATION AND THE RELATIONSHIP BETWEEN THE HIGH SEAS AND THE EEZ

Despite the exclusion of the general provisions of Part VII[12] (on the High Seas) from the EEZ regime, Article 58(1)[13] protects the enjoyment of the freedom of navigation *inter alia* referred to in Article 87.[14] Moreover, Articles 88 to 115[15] of Part VII[16] and other pertinent rules of international law are also applied to the EEZ in so far as they are not incompatible with the EEZ regime.[17] It is noteworthy, however, that despite the inclusion of the freedom of navigation in the EEZ, the quality of this right may not be the same as that enjoyed on the high seas. Although the drafters of UNCLOS imply, through the cross-reference to Article 87,[18] that a vessel traversing in the EEZ of a State enjoys the same quality of navigation, UNCLOS limits this said freedom by imposing the obligation on flag States to pay 'due regard'[19] to the rights and duties of the coastal State as well as to comply with laws and regulations adopted by that State.[20]

1.3 FREEDOM OF NAVIGATION ON THE HIGH SEAS

The high seas freedom of navigation was enunciated in Article 2[21] of the 1958 High Seas Convention and elaborated upon in Article 87.[22] As stated by Beckman and Davenport, 'Article 87 of UNCLOS explicitly recognizes the freedom of navigation as a high seas freedom.'[23] The 1958 HSC is an important source of Article 87[24] and its main text was taken from the International Law Commission's draft Article 27,[25] with several major additions.[26] The importance of the high seas freedom of navigation is also reflected in various UNCLOS III sources.[27]

In terms of Article 90,[28] 'every state whether coastal or land-locked, has the right to sail ships flying its flag on the high seas'.[29] This freedom of navigation on the high seas is limited. In fact, the high seas freedom of navigation, like all the freedoms of the high seas, is subject to general limitations on its exercise.[30] In terms of Article 87(1)[31] the freedoms of the high seas, including the freedom of navigation, must be exercised 'under the conditions laid down by this Convention and by other rules of international law'.[32] These rules include duties relating to the prevention, reduction and control of marine pollution, requirements for the safety of navigation and requirements for the protection of life at sea.[33] The high seas freedom of navigation, unlike other freedoms[34] enumerated in article 87,[35] is not expressly subjected to other specific provisions of UNCLOS, as is the case with other high seas freedoms like for example freedom of fishing.

It is noteworthy that only ships flying the flag of a State enjoy the freedom of navigation on the high seas. Stateless vessels do not enjoy this freedom as it is only given to registered vessels.[36]

1.3.1. The 'Due Regard' Requirement

Article 87(2)[37] together with Article 2[38] of the 1958 HSC further require that States have 'reasonable regard'[39] for the interests of other States in exercising the freedoms of the high seas including the freedom of navigation. The 'reasonable regard'[40] principle is elaborated upon in Article 87(2),[41] which requires States to exercise their navigational freedoms with 'due regard'[42] to the interests of other States. The author is to further emphasize the 'due regard'[43] requirement and indirectly illustrate its importance by exploring some conflicts between weapon testing on the high seas and rights concerning navigation. The 'due regard'[44] principle imposes an obligation on States to exercise high seas freedoms in good faith. Furthermore, Article 300[45] provides that State parties shall fulfil in good faith the obligations assumed under UNCLOS, and shall exercise their rights, jurisdiction and *freedoms* recognised under UNCLOS in a manner which does not constitute an 'abuse of right'.[46]

Warning areas are an example of how the 'due regard'[47] principle works under the law of the sea. Any nation may declare a temporary warning area in international waters and airspace to advise other nations of the conduct of activities that, although lawful, are hazardous to navigation and/or overflight.[48] Other States are not required to remain outside a declared warning area within international waters but may operate therein subject to the requirement of 'due regard'[49] for the rights of the declaring nation to use international waters and airspace for such lawful purposes.[50]

1.3.1.1. The High Seas and Nuclear Weapons Tests

The importance of the 'due regard'[51] requirement may be further exemplified with reference to the use of the high seas for nuclear weapons tests.

Beginning in 1946, the United States conducted nuclear weapons tests on atolls in the Pacific Ocean. The United States Atomic Energy Commission was authorized to establish danger zones and vessels were warned to stay clear of the areas, which covered extensive portions of the high seas. This, of course, greatly restricted the high seas freedom of navigation. In fact, the use of the high seas for nuclear tests caused great controversy[52] and at the First United Nations Law of the Sea Conference, Czechoslovakia, Poland, the former Soviet Union and former Yugoslavia tabled a proposal[53] to include in the 1958 HSC an article[54] stating that States are bound to refrain from testing nuclear weapons on the high seas.[55] Furthermore, India then tabled another proposal[56] in this sense which was overwhelmingly adopted and was not even put to a vote.

The Nuclear Tests Cases (Australia v. France[57] and New Zealand v. France)[58] may also be relevant in this context of 'due regard'.[59] The 'dangerous zones'[60] there declared also extended into the high seas around the atoll and thus posed a threat to the high seas freedom of navigation. In situations like this the 'due regard'[61] requirement becomes very important because it is through the 'due regard'[62] for the rights and duties of other States coupled with the 'due regard'[63] for the rights and duties of the coastal State that the high seas freedom of navigation could be protected.

1.3.2. Ships Engaged in Prohibited Activities

Articles 88 to 115[64] contain a number of provisions restricting the freedom of navigation of States *inter alia* on the high seas. Article 88 of UNCLOS requires that the freedom of navigation may only be used for peaceful purposes and this is in itself another restriction. The freedom of navigation does not extend to Stateless vessels or to vessels that are engaged in certain prohibited activities like piracy,[65] slave trade,[66] unauthorized broadcasting[67] and the illicit traffic in narcotic drugs or psychotropic substances.[68]

1.4 THE HIGH SEAS FREEDOM OF NAVIGATION IN THE EEZ

The cornerstone of the resulting economic zone package is found in two articles, 56[69] and 58,[70] although many other provisions in the Treaty are made relevant through the use of cross-references and placement in the chapter.[71] Article 56,[72] deals 'with the rights and duties of coastal States in the EEZ'.[73] Paragraph 1(a) of Article 56,[74] gives coastal States:

> sovereign rights over three main resources, (1) non-living resources on the seabed, subsoil and superjacent waters, (2) living resources of the seabed, subsoil and superjacent waters and (3) other economic activities related to the economic exploitation and exploration of the zone.[75]

In particular Article 56[76] paragraph 1(a) makes 'two points eminently clear', Clingan states:[77]

> (1) the rights of the coastal state are economic in nature, having to do with resources and resource-related subjects; and (2) these economic rights are exclusive [not preferential] to the coastal state.[78]

In contrast with Article 56, 'Article 58 refers to the rights and freedoms of other states in the EEZ.'[79] The basic rights, unqualified in nature, are 'the freedoms of navigation and overflight referred to in Article 87 and of the laying of submarine cables and pipelines, which are therefore qualitatively the same as when they are exercised in the area seaward of the zone'.[80]

As Article 58 clarifies, 'Article 87 is not incorporated by reference.'[81] This is because Article 87 lists uses[82] that are clearly incompatible with the rights of coastal States in the EEZ. In addition, the high seas freedoms in Article 87[83] are not exclusive.[84] On Article 58 of UNCLOS, Clingan opines that:[85]

> the freedoms of navigation and overflight and the laying of submarine cables and pipelines, without more, was seen as presenting the possibility of a restrictive reading of the article to permit those freedoms and those freedoms only.[86]

Robertson argues that the 'basic regime for navigation in the exclusive economic zone is based upon the 'freedom' of navigation.'[87] This freedom, subject only to the provisions of UNCLOS and 'other rules of international law', is the same as that applicable on the high seas. As already elaborated upon in this chapter the high seas freedom of navigation is not absolute.[88]

The limitations to the high seas freedom of navigation apply also in the EEZ regime. Moreover Article 58[89] makes the freedom of navigation in the EEZ subject to 'the relevant provisions of this Convention'. [90] Furthermore, the 'other internationally lawful uses of the sea related to'[91] the listed uses must be 'compatible with this Convention'.[92] This language is 'foreign to the 1958 Geneva Conventions which, of course, were void of the concept of the EEZ.'[93] Article 58(1)[94] thus provides a two-tier test; it is not enough that the 'other internationally lawful'[95] use be related to for example the freedom of navigation but the 'other internationally lawful'[96] use must as well be 'compatible'[97] with UNCLOS. In addition, as Article 58(2)[98] states 'articles 88 to 115 of the high seas and other pertinent rules of international law apply to the exclusive economic zone only if not incompatible with this [EEZ] Part'.[99] This compatibility requirement is 'beneficial because it provides necessary balance'.[100] Some of the high seas rights in articles 88 to 115[101] can easily be applied in an EEZ context without compatibility being an issue. In clearer terms some of the rights contained in articles 88 to 115[102] may practically be applied in the EEZ. This is true with 'universal'[103] provisions of UNCLOS like those concerning piracy[104] , nationality of ships[105] and proscription against subjecting any part of the high seas to sovereignty.[106] However, other UNCLOS provisions may raise a compatibility problem if strictly applied in the EEZ. Article 110[107] is one such provision which spells out the circumstances under which vessels may be approached and boarded when on the high seas. In the case of Article 110,[108] incompatibility in the EEZ may arise because the EEZ part 'provides for additional boarding rights,[109] such as for fisheries enforcement'.[110]

Article 58(3)[111] is a further restriction but is not 'a limitation on the rights specified in article 58...only a limitation upon the manner in which those rights are to be exercised'.[112]

1.4.1. Additional Limitations in the EEZ

It may be argued that Article 58(3)[113] creates two additional sources of legal limitations on the high seas freedom of navigation in the EEZ beyond those existent on the high seas. Robertson refers to the two sources as 'incompatible uses authorized or actually conducted by the coastal State'[114] and 'laws and regulations adopted by the coastal State'[115] that directly or indirectly affect the freedom of navigation in the EEZ.[116]

1.4.1.1. Incompatible Uses

The so called problem of 'incompatible uses'[117] can arise either from uses that were foreseen and are thus specifically provided for in UNCLOS[118] or by uses that although not specifically listed in UNCLOS may fit within the 'other activities for the economic exploitation and exploration of the zone'[119] part of Article 56[120] cited above.

For current or foreseen uses, UNCLOS attempts to prescribe limits on the competence of the coastal State to ensure that the exercise of its rights did not interfere with the rights that other States can exercise in the EEZ. An example of this would be the right of the coastal State to construct, and to authorize and regulate the construction, operation and use of artificial islands, installations and other structures in the EEZ.[121] For this right UNCLOS specifies measures to safeguard the freedom of navigation and other lawful activities in the EEZ. It should be noted that the coastal State's exclusive authority with respect to artificial islands is not explicitly limited to artificial islands constructed for the purposes provided for in Article 56[122] or other economic purposes.[123] This limitation applies only to installations and structures.[124] Article 60[125] specifies the safeguards to protect the rights of other States in the EEZ from interference by the coastal State. Upon the construction of these installations and structures a coastal State is obliged by UNCLOS to provide due notice of their construction but also give warning of their presence and remove them when their use is no longer required.[126] Coastal States may establish reasonable safety zones around these installations and structures but the zones may not exceed a specified size and international standards must be kept in mind.[127] Furthermore, artificial islands, installations and structures may not be constructed in areas where they will interfere with 'recognized sea lanes essential to international navigation'.[128] In addition to all these explicit restrictions the coastal State shall have 'due regard to the rights and duties of other States in the exclusive economic zone'.[129]

Less straightforward are uses that are not foreseen in UNCLOS. The situation is less clear when the coastal State is asserting:

> a sovereign right for the purpose of exploring and exploiting, conserving and managing the natural resources, whether living or non-living or with regard to other activities for the economic exploitation and exploration of the zone.[130]

This notwithstanding the fact that UNCLOS provides more specific detail in respect of some of these rights. The 'conservation of living resources'[131] is one example of the latter rights which is specifically dealt with in Article 61[132] cited below:

> 1. The coastal State shall determine the *allowable catch of the living resources* in its exclusive economic zone.
>
> 2. The coastal State, taking into account the best scientific evidence available to it, shall ensure through proper conservation and management measures that the *maintenance of the living resources* in the exclusive economic zone is not endangered by over-exploitation. As appropriate, the coastal State and

competent international organizations, whether subregional, regional or global, shall cooperate to this end.

3. Such measures shall also be designed to *maintain or restore populations* of harvested species at levels which can produce the maximum sustainable yield, as qualified by relevant environmental and economic factors, including the economic needs of coastal fishing communities and the special requirements of developing States, and taking into account fishing patterns, the interdependence of stocks and any generally recommended international minimum standards, whether subregional, regional or global.

4. In taking such measures the coastal State shall take into consideration the effects on species associated with or dependent upon harvested species with a view to *maintaining or restoring populations* of such associated or dependent species above levels at which their reproduction may become seriously threatened.

5. Available scientific information, catch and fishing effort statistics, and other data relevant to the conservation of fish stocks shall be contributed and exchanged on a regular basis through competent international organizations, whether subregional, regional or global, where appropriate and with participation by all States concerned, including States whose nationals are allowed to fish in the exclusive economic zone.[133]

Some may argue that 'conservation'[134] relates to the protection of the marine environment from pollution. However, the author agrees with Robertson[135] that Article 61[136] limits 'conservation'[137] to measures the coastal State may take in relation to the bolded phrases in the above cited text.[138] This because Article 61[139] seems to spell out what measures the coastal State may take to conserve its natural resources in the EEZ.

Coastal States have wide room for discretion under the general rights of 'economic exploration and exploitation'[140] of the EEZ. However, in relation to unforeseen uses the treaty-makers provided a set of generic procedures and criteria in order to resolve any conflicts that might occur. So other States can protect their right of navigation in the EEZ by resorting to any of three UNCLOS tools: (i) Article 56[141] and its 'due regard'[142] requirement; (ii) the 'residual rights'[143] of Article 59[144] and (iii) the right to use the compulsory dispute-settlement processes provided in Part XV.[145]

1.4.1.2. Priority Between Competing Uses

UNCLOS establishes no priority between the rights of the coastal State and the rights of other States in the EEZ. However, at times priority may be argued to be natural. If for example, a coastal State builds an artificial structure in the EEZ it may be argued that naturally the use of that artificial structure takes priority over the right of navigation through the spot of that structure. Article 60(7)[146] expressly provides that if there exists a recognized sea lane essential to international navigation, the sea lane has priority over artificial structures and installations. Thus a coastal State may not establish an artificial structure there.

In terms of Articles 56[147] and 58[148] both the coastal State and other States must have 'due regard'[149] for the competing rights of each other. In addition, coastal States must act in a manner 'compatible with the provisions of this Convention'[150] while other States must comply with the 'laws and regulations adopted by the coastal State in accordance with the provisions of this Convention and other rules of international law in so far as they are not incompatible with this Part'.[151] The other States' interests give way only in so far as the coastal State is given prescriptive competence by UNCLOS itself or other rules of international law.[152] As Oxman puts it 'these balanced duties will provide the juridical basis for resolving many practical problems of competing uses'.[153]

1.4.1.3. Residual Rights

It is when priority is not generalized and/or UNCLOS does not provide for a specific use that Article 59[154] and its 'residual rights'[155] enter into the picture. Article 59[156] states that:

> In cases where this Convention does not attribute rights or jurisdiction to the coastal State or to other States within the exclusive economic zone, and a conflict arises between the interests of the coastal State and any other State or States, the conflict should be resolved on the basis of equity and in the light of all the relevant circumstances, taking into account the respective importance of the interests involved to the parties as well as to the international community as a whole.[157]

When the rights of other States in the EEZ come in conflict with the rights of the coastal State in the EEZ the conflict should be resolved on the basis of equity.[158] It may be argued that in public international law equity is an established legal concept and has its own meaning. Furthermore, the interests of the 'international community as a whole'[159] must be taken into consideration. This final criterion makes a lot of sense especially when considering that the international community as a whole has a major interest in the EEZ – an area that embraces over thirty-five percent of the world's oceans.[160]

1.4.1.4. Naval Manoeuvres

An important interest to some maritime States that may be argued to be incompatible with the rights of coastal States in the EEZ is the right to conduct naval manoeuvres.[161] Richardson and Clingan[162] argue strongly that the high seas freedom of navigation includes the right to conduct military manoeuvres and exercises whilst respecting the 'due regard'[163] for the rights of other States exercising their freedoms of the high seas.

It can be convincingly argued that Article 88[164], which is also applicable in the EEZ, limits the right of naval manoeuvres in the EEZ. Article 88[165] reserves the high seas for peaceful purposes. For the scope of this book it is sufficient to observe that if 'peaceful purposes'[166] restricts naval manoeuvres in the EEZ it equally does so on the high seas.

1.4.1.5. Coastal State Laws and Regulations

Coastal State laws and regulations, as will be examined in this section, may directly or indirectly affect the high seas freedom of navigation in the EEZ. These laws and regulations can in themselves restrict the freedom of navigation in the EEZ beyond the limitations existent on the freedom of navigation on the high seas. The author is to divide coastal State laws and regulations in two classes mainly (i) laws and regulations coming from explicit powers in UNCLOS and (ii) laws and regulations promulgated by the coastal State through powers implied in UNCLOS. Article 60(4)[167] is the only provision in the whole UNCLOS which explicitly empowers the coastal State to regulate navigation in the EEZ. Article 60(4)[168] states that:

> The coastal State may, where necessary, establish reasonable safety zones around such artificial islands, installations and structures in which it may take appropriate measures to ensure the safety both of navigation and of the artificial islands, installations and structures.[169]

The article gives no definition of 'appropriate measures'.[170] However, Article 60[171] itself contains various restrictions on the size of the safety zones and on the placement of the structures so as to eliminate unnecessary interference by the coastal State with the high seas freedom of navigation in the EEZ.[172] Furthermore, Article 60(7)[173] prohibits the establishment of installations and structures 'where interference may be caused to the use of recognized sea lanes essential to international navigation'.[174] All these limitations on the coastal State's explicit empowerment of Article 60(4)[175] greatly limit the negative impact a coastal State may leave on the freedom of navigation in the EEZ.

Article 58(3)[176] obliges other States to comply with the 'laws and regulations adopted by the coastal State in accordance with the provisions of UNCLOS and other rules of international law in so far as they are not incompatible with this Part'.[177] Although these 'laws and regulations'[178] may not be aimed at controlling the freedom of navigation, their implementation may indirectly have that effect. Abuse of the powers by coastal States could pose a serious danger to the freedom of navigation in the EEZ.[179] In this regard the protection and preservation of the marine environment is the most significant example of such regulatory power. This book will devote a part of this chapter to pollution control in the EEZ and how this can limit the high seas freedom of navigation in the EEZ.[180]

Article 56[181] gives coastal States sovereign rights for the purpose of 'exploring and exploiting, conserving and managing the natural resources'[182] of the EEZ. This competence might give rise to regulations by the coastal State that limit the freedom of navigation in the EEZ. This might for example happen due to coastal State regulations that excessively conserve and manage the natural resources of the coastal State in the EEZ. Such regulations may thus restrict, perhaps severely, the freedom of navigation in the EEZ.

1.4.1.6. The Fisheries Articles of UNCLOS Part V[183]

Coastal States are given various implied powers in relation to the conservation and utilisation of living resources under Part V.[184] In particular, Article 62[185] provides that other States fishing in the EEZ must 'comply with the conservation measures and with other laws and conditions established in the laws and regulations of the coastal State'.[186] Article 73[187] is also very relevant in this context. These powers that UNCLOS grants to the coastal State when fishing in the EEZ may in a sense affect the freedom of navigation in the EEZ, at least as far as fishing vessels are concerned. It very much depends on the interpretation given to Article 73.[188] For example, it may be argued that Article 73[189] permits coastal States to only board and inspect fishing vessels. However, others may argue that any vessel falls within Article 73.[190]

Burke[191] argues that in some situations navigational interests must give way, however, this is only done in exceptional circumstances and in a very limited manner. Burke's 'exceptional circumstances'[192] would only occur in the case of a few small nations whose dependence on the exploitation of coastal fisheries is vital to national well-being and enforcement of restrictions is difficult yet critical to effective management.[193] According to Burke the effect on the freedom of navigation would have to be minimal and the benefits of better compliance and enforcement would have to outweigh.[194] In Burke's opinion the limited authority he would permit to be exercised under these exceptional circumstances would rule out measures that are the equivalent of a territorial-sea regime, or that would bar the entry of fishing vessels without specific authority, or that would require the carriage and use of transponders.[195] However, Burke's limited authority would in specific situations permit requiring adherence to sea lanes, stowage of fishing gear or reporting of entry and exit and route used.[196] In this regard the author strongly agrees with Burke. The author believes that freedom of navigation should be the rule and whilst exceptional circumstances should be catered for, caveats have to be in place so as to safeguard the high seas freedom of navigation in the EEZ.

It is true that UNCLOS grants powers to the coastal State which may indirectly have a bearing on the freedom of navigation in the EEZ. However, the author agrees with Robertson that the burden of proving necessity for regulation and the particular measures of control adopted should rest on the coastal State.[197] By adopting such measures the coastal State may restrict the freedom of navigation in the EEZ and this should require some justification in the interests of the freedom of navigation itself.

1.4.1.7. Protection and Preservation of the Marine Environment

Article 211(5)[198] permits the coastal State to adopt laws and regulations for the prevention, reduction and control of pollution in the EEZ.[199] This coastal State's competence to preserve and protect the marine environment may be argued to be one of the most serious potential threats to the freedom of navigation in the EEZ.[200] It may be argued that the competence of Article 211(5)[201] could indirectly control the high seas freedom of navigation in the EEZ. In fact, at least in the early stages of UNCLOS III, some maritime States were wary of giving very broad powers to coastal States over vessel-source pollution.[202] Instead, they preferred to reinforce existing flag State schemes.[203] However, the *Amoco Cadiz* disaster[204] resulted in a more general consensus to recognize the concerns of coastal States in protecting the resources of the EEZ from the dangers of vessel-source pollution.[205]

As far as marine pollution control is concerned Article 56(1)(b)(iii)[206] is of crucial importance. With regard to the protection and preservation of the marine environment,[207] this article grants coastal States jurisdiction 'as provided for in the relevant provisions'[208] of UNCLOS. *Prima facie* it results that Article 56(1)(b)(iii)[209] uses the 'relevant provisions'[210] of UNCLOS to limit the coastal State's jurisdiction to protect the marine environment. The actual powers granted to the coastal State are found in other 'relevant provisions'[211] of UNCLOS. Part XII[212] contains the 'relevant provisions'[213] for vessels exercising freedom of navigation and other uses associated with the operations of ships and aircraft. Briefly, this Part XII[214] provides a system of prescriptive and enforcement jurisdictions for the purposes of vessel-source pollution.

For UNCLOS's anti-pollution framework to work properly coastal States and flag States must fulfil their obligations under UNCLOS.[215] In fact the coastal State's competence to exercise prescriptive and enforcement jurisdiction in the EEZ is only permitted if that competence is qualified by 'numerous checks and balances against arbitrary and unfair actions'.[216] Other States may only exercise freedom of navigation in the EEZ, if flag States have the obligation to enforce international standards for less serious violations.[217] Moreover the coastal States themselves must have the right of direct intervention in cases of more serious violations else the freedom of navigation of other States in the EEZ would not be permitted.[218]

The prescriptive jurisdiction of the coastal State in the promulgation of laws and regulations within the EEZ is dealt with in Article 211.[219] Its part (5)[220] provides that:

> Coastal States, for the purpose of enforcement as provided for in section 6, may in respect of their exclusive economic zones adopt laws and regulations for the prevention, reduction and control of pollution from vessels conforming to and giving effect to generally accepted international rules and standards established through the competent international organization or general diplomatic conference.[221]

The article grants prescriptive jurisdiction to the coastal State to adopt regulations for the prevention, reduction and control of pollution, however, with the limitation that any laws or regulations adopted must conform 'to generally accepted international rules and standards'.[222] No self-made standards are thus accepted in the EEZ. It is important to note that Article 211(5)[223] grants the coastal State a wide prescriptive jurisdiction but the enforcement jurisdiction is not co-extensive with that prescriptive jurisdiction.[224]

The coastal State may only take direct enforcement action if the pollution threat exceeds a certain limit. In respect of violations that do not exceed this limit, the coastal State's action on vessels navigating in its EEZ is restricted to requiring the vessel to give information.[225] Follow-up enforcement action then falls within the competence of the flag State or port State to which the coastal State reports the relevant information.[226] The 'relevant provisions'[227] allow no instance of interference with the freedom of navigation in the EEZ in cases of minor violations.

However, as Robertson argues, there are three specific circumstances in which the coastal State is allowed to take enforcement action on violations of its anti-pollution regulations in the EEZ.[228] The first 'circumstance'[229] is where the ship is in an off-shore terminal within the EEZ and this is dealt with in Article 218(1)[230] in conjunction with Article 219.[231] The second instance is that of Article 220(5).[232] The coastal State may take direct enforcement action when there are clear grounds for believing that a vessel navigating in the EEZ committed a violation like in the first circumstance above and the violation results 'in a substantial discharge causing or threating significant pollution of the marine environment'.[233] Article 220(6)[234] gives the third scenario of 'clear objective evidence'[235] that a vessel navigating in the EEZ has committed a violation as described in the other 'circumstances'[236] and the violation has resulted 'in a discharge causing major damage or threat of major damage…".[237] The enforcement competence of coastal States in the EEZ is limited by various caveats. Many UNCLOS provisions restrict the coastal State's action so to protect the freedom of navigation in the EEZ from physical interference or interruption. Such provisions include Articles 224,[238] 225,[239] 226(1)(a),[240] 226(1)(b),[241] and 227.[242] Apart from this, other provisions in UNCLOS ensure due process rights for all parties concerned in the investigation and institution of proceedings in an enforcement process.[243] Prime examples are Articles 228(1),[244] 228(2),[245] 228(3),[246] 230(1),[247] 230(3)[248] and 231.[249] These articles provide examples of procedural protections, which are required because unfair procedures and/or penalties could pose a threat to navigation in the EEZ by rendering it more burdensome or expensive.[250]

1.4.1.8. Ice-Covered Areas

Another UNCLOS section about pollution control that may also impact navigation in the EEZ is Article 234[251] which regulates ice-covered areas. The coastal State must stick to only adopting regulations that are 'non-discriminatory'[252] and have 'due regard to navigation and the protection and preservation of the marine environment based on the best available scientific evidence'.[253] The author agrees with Robertson[254] that Article 234[255] creates room for abuse and arbitrary action against vessels in 'ice-covered areas'[256] when compared to enforcement in the EEZ in general. Fortunately, ice-covered areas like the Arctic do not embrace many of the major international sea lanes.[257]

1.4.1.9. Pollution from Vessels and Sovereign Immunity

In this context both Articles 211[258] and 236[259] deserve some brief mention. Article 211[260] grants coastal States a competence similar to that of Article 234[261] but in more restricted terms and in relation to clearly defined areas in the EEZ. For such areas Article 211[262] allows stricter standards than the generally accepted international ones. However, to prevent arbitrary rules and regulations whilst protecting the high seas freedom of navigation in the EEZ, such stricter standards must be approved by the competent international organization. Article 236[263] exempts 'warships, naval auxiliaries, other vessels'[264] 'owned or operated by a State and used'[265] only on 'government non-commercial service'[266] from the application of any UNCLOS provisions on marine protection. However, the same article obliges States to adopt appropriate measures to ensure that such vessels 'act in a manner consistent, so far as is reasonable and practicable, with the Convention'.[267]

As a whole, the pollution provisions in UNCLOS 'place a premium upon the viability of navigation within the economic zone, yet allow reasonable protection to the coastal state'.[268]

1.4.1.10. Marine Scientific Research

It is proper to add that the marine scientific research provisions contained in Part XIII[269] may also impact the high seas freedom of navigation in the EEZ. In fact, Clingan writes that the impact can 'clearly be true of the conduct of marine scientific research'.[270]

1.4.1.11. Dispute Settlement Mechanism

For the sake of completion, it must be added that if coastal States interfere with the high seas freedom of navigation in the EEZ, other States whose vessels are affected, may have recourse to the compulsory dispute settlement mechanism[271] of UNCLOS. Unfortunately, a detailed discussion on the dispute settlement mechanism is beyond the scope of this book.[272]

1.5 CONCLUSION

The 'sovereign rights'[273] granted to coastal States in the EEZ brought about the possibility of 'conflicts with the community interests of navigation'.[274] Hence, UNCLOS provides for an 'interlocking web of relationships'[275] between the coastal States, other States and international institutions like the IMO.[276] It results that the high seas freedom of navigation is not absolute, yet in the EEZ it is subject to greater limitations than on the high seas. The 'due regard'[277] limitation is perhaps one of the most noteworthy limitations. Coastal States cannot separate their right to EEZ resources from their duty to have 'due regard'[278] to the right of other States to navigate freely within the EEZ.[279] The detailed regime found in UNCLOS appears reasonably adequate to protect the high seas freedom of navigation within the EEZ. However, certain difficulties may arise. For example, it may be argued that under UNCLOS it is not clear how extensive the rights of warships are.[280] 'Can warships engage in naval manoeuvres or practise using their weapons?'[281] Although these military uses may be considered as 'uses of the sea related to'[282] navigation, their lawfulness and compatibility with 'other UNCLOS provisions'[283] particularly with UNCLOS Article 88 may be disputed.

NOTES

1. Rüdiger Wolfrum, "Freedom of Navigation: New Challenges" (International Tribunal for the Law of the Sea) 2; see in general Rüdiger Wolfrum, "The Freedom of Navigation: Modern Challenges" in Lilian del Castillo, *Law of the Sea, From Grotius to the International Tribunal for the Law of the Sea* (Brill Nijhoff, 2015) 89-103; see also in general Hasjim Dalal, "The Law of the Sea Convention and Navigational Freedoms" in Donald R. Rothwell and Sam Bateman, *Navigational Rights and Freedoms and the Law of the Sea* (Martinus Nijhoff Publishers, 2000) 1-10.

2. De Jure Praedae of 1609.

3. Rüdiger Wolfrum (n 1) 2; for the principle of Freedom of Navigation see Michael A. Becker, "The Shifting Public Order of the Oceans: Freedom of Navigation and the Interdiction at Sea" *Harvard International Law Journal* 46 (2005) 131-230; see also Cord-Georg Hasselmann, *Die Freiheit der Handelsschiffahrt: Eine Analyse der UN-Seerechtskonvention* (N.P. Engel, 1987).

4. Rules applicable to all ships regarding innocent passage in the territorial sea; see UNCLOS, Part II, Section 3, Articles 17-26.

5. High seas routes or routes through exclusive economic zones through straits used for international navigation; see the UNCLOS, Part III, Section 1, Article 36.

6. Right of transit passage; see UNCLOS, Part III, Section 2, Article 38.

7. Right of innocent passage; see the UNCLOS, Part IV, Article 52.

8. Rights and duties of other States in the exclusive economic zone; see UNCLOS, Part IV, Article 58.

9. Legal status of the superjacent waters and air space and the rights and freedoms of other States; see UNCLOS, Part VI, Article 78.

10. Freedom of the high seas; see UNCLOS, Part VII, Section 1, Article 87.

11. Rüdiger Wolfrum (n 1) 2.

12. UNCLOS, Part VII, Sections 1-2, Articles 86-120.

13. Ibid, Part V, Article 58(1).

14. 1. The high seas are open to all States, whether coastal or land-locked. Freedom of the high seas is exercised under the conditions laid down by this Convention and by other rules of international law. It comprises, *inter alia*, both for coastal and land-locked States:

(a) *freedom of navigation*;

(b) freedom of overflight;

(c) freedom to lay submarine cables and pipelines, subject to Part VI;

(d) freedom to construct artificial islands and other installations permitted under international law, subject to Part VI;

(e) freedom of fishing, subject to the conditions laid down in section 2;

(f) freedom of scientific research, subject to Parts VI and XIII.

2. These freedoms shall be exercised by all States with due regard for the interests of other States in their exercise of the freedom of the high seas, and also with due regard for the rights under this Convention with respect to activities in the Area; UNCLOS, Part VII, Section 1, Article 87.

15. Ibid, Article 88-115.

16. Ibid, Sections 1-2, Articles 86-120.

17. UNCLOS, Part V, Article 58(2).

18. Ibid, Article 87.

19. Ibid.

20. UNCLOS, Part V, Article 58(3).

21. The high seas being open to all nations, no State may validly purport to subject any part of them to its sovereignty. Freedom of the high seas is exercised under the conditions laid down by these articles and by the other rules of international law. It comprises, inter alia, both for coastal and non-coastal States:

(1) *Freedom of navigation*;

(2) Freedom of fishing;

(3) Freedom to lay submarine cables and pipelines;

(4) Freedom to fly over the high seas.

These freedoms, and others which are recognized by the general principles of international law, shall be exercised by all States with reasonable regard to the interests of other States in their exercise of the freedom of the high seas; see the 1958 HSC, Article 2.

22. UNCLOS, Part VII, Section 1, Article 87.

23. Robert Beckman, and Tara Davenport, "The EEZ Regime: Reflections after 30 Years" [2012] LOSI Conference Papers 1, 2.

24. UNCLOS, Part VII, Section 1, Article 87.

25. Report of the International Law Commission covering the work of its eighth session, article 27 (ILC, 1956) 253, 278.

26. The opening paragraph added the second sentence, referring to the exercise of the freedom of the high seas 'under the conditions laid down by these articles and by the other rules of international law' based on proposal UN Doc. A/CONF.13/C.2/L.3 (1958) by Mexico; the reference to the freedom of the high seas applying 'both for coastal and for non-coastal States' was adopted by the Fifth Committee based on proposal UN Doc. A/CONF.13/C.5/L.15 (1958) by Switzerland; the paragraph following the list of freedoms was also added, to provide a test of reasonableness in the exercise by all States of their freedom of the high seas based on

proposal UN Doc. A/CONF.13/C.2/L.68 (1958) by the United Kingdom; in combination with the addition in the opening paragraph, the text emphasizes that the exercise by a State of the freedom of the high seas carries with it certain obligations; see also John Norton Moore, Myron H. Nordquist, Satya N. Nandan and Shabtai Rosenne, *United Nations Convention on the Law of the Sea 1982: A Commentary* (Martinus Nijhoff Publishers, 1993), Volume VII 72.

27. The most relevant sources include proposal UN Doc. A/A.138/SC.II/L.45 (1973) by China, working paper UN Doc. A/CONF.62/C.2/L.68 (1974) by El Salvador and proposal UN Doc. A/AC.138/SC.II/L.21 by Columbia, Mexico and Venezuela; see also John Norton Moore, Myron H. Nordquist, Satya N. Nandan and Shabtai Rosenne (n 26) Volume VII 73-86.

28. Ibid, Article 90.

29. Ibid.

30. See Chapter 1, Section 1.3.1.

31. Ibid, Article 87(1).

32. Ibid.

33. John Norton Moore, Myron H. Nordquist, Satya N. Nandan and Shabtai Rosenne (n 26) Volume III 81.

34. For example, the freedom of scientific research is expressly subjected to Parts VI and XIII of the UNCLOS, the freedom of fishing is explicitly subjected to the conditions laid down in section 2 and the freedom to lay submarine cables and pipelines is expressly subjected to the UNCLOS Part VI; see UNCLOS, Part VII, Article 87(1).

35. Ibid, Part VII, Section 1, Article 87.

36. See David Joseph Attard and Patricia Mallia, "The High Seas" in David Joseph Attard, Malgosia Fitzmaurice and Norman A. Martínez Gutiérrez, *The IMLI Manual on International Maritime Law* (Oxford University Press, 2014) 239-275.

37. Ibid. Article 87(2).

38. 1958 HSC, Article 2.

39. Ibid.

40. Ibid.

41. UNCLOS, Part VII, Section 1, Article 87(2).

42. Ibid.

43. Ibid.

44. Ibid.

45. Ibid, Part XVI, Article 300.

46. Ibid.

47. Ibid, Part VII, Section 1, Article 87(2).

48. The United States, for example, routinely declares such areas for missile testing, gunnery exercises, space vehicle recovery operations and other purposes entailing some danger to other lawful uses of the high seas by other States; see A. R. Thomas and James C. Duncan, "Annotated Supplement to The Commander's Handbook on the Law of Naval Operations" *International Law Studies* 73 (1999) 99.

49. UNCLOS, Part VII, Section 1, Article 87(2).

50. A. R. Thomas and James C. Duncan (n 48) 99.

51. UNCLOS, Part VII, Section 1, Article 87(2).

52. The controversy was about the use of the high seas for nuclear weapons tests, which tests led to extensive portions of the high seas being established as danger zones with the consequence of severely restricting the freedom of navigation therein.

53. Proposal UN Doc. A/CONF.13/C.2/L.30 by Czechoslovakia, Poland, the Soviet Union and Yugoslavia.

54. The article stated that "States are bound to refrain from testing nuclear weapons on the high seas."; see Proposal UN Doc. A/CONF.13/C.2/L.30 by Czechoslovakia, Poland, the Soviet Union and Yugoslavia; see also Louis B. Sohn, John E. Noyes, Erik Franckx and Kristen G. Juras, *Cases and Materials on the Law of the Sea* (Martinus Nijhoff, 2014) 43–101.

55. Louis B. Sohn, John E. Noyes, Erik Franckx and Kristen G. Juras (n 54) 43–101.

56. Proposal UN Doc. A/CONF.13/C.2/L.71 by India.

57. *Nuclear Tests Case (Australia v France)* (Merits) [1974] ICJ Rep 253.

58. *Nuclear Tests Case (New Zealand v France)* (Merits) [1974] ICJ Rep 457.

59. UNCLOS, Part VII, Section 1, Article 87(2). For the whole facts and legal principles in detail see Louis B. Sohn, John E. Noyes, Erik Franckx and Kristen G. Juras (n 54) 43-101.
60. Ibid.
61. UNCLOS, Part VII, Section 1, Article 87(2).
62. Ibid.
63. Ibid.
64. Ibid, Articles 88 to 115.
65. Ibid, Article 100.
66. Ibid, Article 99.
67. Ibid, Article 109.
68. Ibid, Article 108.
69. Ibid, Part V, Article 56.
70. Ibid, Article 58
71. Thomas A. Clingan, "Freedom of Navigation in a Post-UNCLOS III Environment" Law and Contemporary Problems 46 (1983) 107-123.
72. 1. In the exclusive economic zone, the coastal State has:

(a) *sovereign rights* for the purpose of exploring and exploiting, conserving and managing the natural resources, whether living or non-living, of the waters superjacent to the seabed and of the seabed and its subsoil, and with regard to other activities for the economic exploitation and exploration of the zone, such as the production of energy from the water, currents and winds;

(b) *jurisdiction* as provided for in the relevant provisions of this Convention with regard to:

(i) the establishment and use of artificial islands, installations and structures;

(ii) marine scientific research;

(iii) the protection and preservation of the marine environment;

(c) *other rights and duties* provided for in this Convention.

2. In exercising its rights and performing its duties under this Convention in the exclusive economic zone, the coastal State shall have *due regard* to the rights and duties of other States and shall act in a manner *compatible with the provisions of this Convention.*

3. The rights set out in this article with respect to the seabed and subsoil shall be exercised in accordance with Part VI; see UNCLOS, Part V, Article 56.

73. Thomas A. Clingan (n 71) 107-123.
74. Ibid.
75. Robert Beckman, and Tara Davenport (n 23) 2.
76. UNCLOS, Part V, Article 56.
77. Thomas A. Clingan (n 71) 107-123.
78. Ibid.
79. Ibid.
80. Ibid.
81. Thomas A. Clingan (n 71) 107-123.
82. For example, fishing.
83. UNCLOS, Part VII, Section 1, Article 87.
84. The phrase *inter alia* makes this clear.
85. UNCLOS, Part V, Article 58.
86. Thomas A. Clingan (n 71) 107-123.
87. Horace B. Robertson, "Navigation in the Exclusive Economic Zone" *Virginia Journal of International Law* 24 (1984) 865.
88. See Chapter 1, Section 1.3.
89. UNCLOS, Part V, Article 58.
90. Ibid.
91. Ibid. Article 58(1).
92. Ibid.
93. Thomas A. Clingan (n 71) 107-123.
94. UNCLOS, Part V, Article 58(1).
95. Ibid.
96. Ibid.

97. Ibid.
98. Ibid.
99. Ibid.
100. Thomas A. Clingan (n 71) 107-123.
101. UNCLOS, Part VII, Section 1, Articles 88 to 115.
102. Ibid.
103. Thomas A. Clingan (n 71) 107-123.
104. UNCLOS, Part VII, Section 1, Articles 100-107.
105. Ibid, Articles 91-93.
106. Ibid, Article 89.
107. Ibid. Article 110.
108. Ibid.
109. Ibid, Part V, Article 73.
110. Thomas A. Clingan (n 71) 107-123.
111. In exercising their rights and performing their duties under this Convention in the exclusive economic zone, States shall have *due regard* to the rights and duties of the coastal State and shall comply with the *laws and regulations adopted by the coastal State* in accordance with the provisions of this Convention and other rules of international law in so far as they are not incompatible with this Part; see UNCLOS, Part V, Article 58(3).
112. Thomas A. Clingan (n 71) 107-123.
113. Ibid.
114. Horace B. Robertson (n 87) 865.
115. UNCLOS, Part V, Article 58(3).
116. Horace B. Robertson (n 87) 865.
117. Ibid.
118. The construction of artificial islands or other structures in the EEZ is for example a foreseen use and is thus specifically provided for in the UNCLOS.
119. UNCLOS, Part V, Article 56.
120. Ibid.
121. UNCLOS, Part V, Article 60.
122. Ibid, Article 56.
123. Horace B. Robertson (n 87) 865.
124. Ibid.
125. UNCLOS, Part V, Article 60.
126. Ibid.
127. Ibid.
128. Ibid, Article 60(7).
129. UNCLOS, Part V, Article 56.
130. Ibid.
131. UNCLOS, Part V, Article 61.
132. Ibid.
133. Ibid.
134. UNCLOS, Part V, Article 56.
135. Horace B. Robertson (n 87) 865.
136. UNCLOS, Part V, Article 61.
137. UNCLOS, Part V, Article 56.
138. For ease of reference the phrases italicised by the author in article 61 are 'allowable catch of the living resources', 'maintenance of the living resources', 'maintain or restore populations' and 'maintaining or restoring populations'.
139. UNCLOS, Part V, Article 61.
140. Ibid, Article 56.
141. Ibid.
142. Ibid.
143. Ibid, Article 59.
144. Ibid.
145. Ibid, Part XV, Articles 279-299.

146. Ibid, Part V, Article 60(7).
147. Ibid, Article 56.
148. Ibid, Article 58.
149. Ibid; see also Article 56.
150. Ibid, Part V, Article 56.
151. UNCLOS, Part V, Article 58.
152. Horace B. Robertson (n 87) 865.
153. Bernard H. Oxman, "The Third United Nations Conference on the Law of the Sea: the 1976 New York Session" *American Journal of International Law* 72 (1977) 260-261.
154. UNCLOS, Part V, Article 59.
155. Ibid.
156. Ibid.
157. Ibid.
158. Ibid.
159. Ibid.
160. Horace B. Robertson (n 87) 865.
161. Ibid.
162. Elliot Richardson, "Law of the Sea: Navigation and Other Traditional Security Considerations" San Diego Law Review 19 (1982) 574; see also Bernard H. Oxman, "An Analysis of the Exclusive Economic Zone as formulated in the Informal Composite Negotiating Text" in Thomas A. Clingan, *Law of the Sea: State Practice in Zones of Special Jurisdiction* (Honolulu Law of the Sea Institute, 1982) 72.
163. UNCLOS, Part V, Article 56.
164. UNCLOS, Part VII, Section 1, Article 88.
165. Ibid.
166. Ibid.
167. UNCLOS, Part V, Article 60(4).
168. Ibid.
169. Ibid.
170. Ibid.
171. Ibid.
172. Horace B. Robertson (n 87) 865.
173. UNCLOS, Part V, Article 60(7).
174. Ibid.
175. Ibid, Part V, Article 60(4).
176. Ibid, Part V, Article 58.
177. Ibid.
178. Ibid.
179. Horace B. Robertson (n 87) 865.
180. See Chapter 1, Section 1.4.1.4.2.
181. UNCLOS, Part V, Article 56.
182. Ibid.
183. See in general Mohamed Dahmani, *The Fisheries Regime of the Exclusive Economic Zone* (Martinus Nijhoff Publishers, 1987); see also Parzival Copes, "The Impact of UNCLOS III on Management of the World's Fisheries" *Marine Policy* 5 (1981) 217-228; see also José Antonio de Yturriaga, *The International Regime of Fisheries: From UNCLOS 1982 to the Presential Sea* (Martinus Nijhoff Publishers, 1997).
184. UNCLOS, Part V, Articles 61-73.
185. Ibid, Article 62.
186. Ibid.
187. 1. The coastal State may, in the exercise of its sovereign rights to explore, exploit, conserve and manage the living resources in the exclusive economic zone, take such measures, including boarding, inspection, arrest and judicial proceedings, as may be necessary to ensure compliance with the *laws and regulations adopted by it* in conformity with this Convention.

2. Arrested vessels and their crews shall be promptly released upon the posting of reasonable bond or other security.

3. Coastal State penalties for violations of fisheries laws and regulations in the exclusive economic zone may not include imprisonment, in the absence of agreements to the contrary by the States concerned, or any other form of corporal punishment.

4. In cases of arrest or detention of foreign vessels the coastal State shall promptly notify the flag State, through appropriate channels, of the action taken and of any penalties subsequently imposed; see Ibid, Article 73.

188. Ibid.
189. Ibid.
190. Ibid.
191. William Burke, "Exclusive Fisheries Zones and Freedom of Navigation" *San Diego Law Review* 20 (1983) 595-623.
192. Ibid.
193. Horace B. Robertson (n 87) 865.
194. William Burke (n 191) 595-623.
195. Horace B. Robertson (n 87) 865.
196. Ibid.
197. Horace B. Robertson (n 87) 865.
198. UNCLOS, Part XII, Section 5, Article 211(5).
199. Thomas A. Clingan (n 71) 107-123.
200. Horace B. Robertson (n 87) 865.
201. UNCLOS, Part XII, Section 5, Article 211(5).
202. Horace B. Robertson (n 87) 865.
203. Ibid.
204. This incident occurred during the UNCLOS III conference. *Amoco Cadiz* was a large crude carrier, on 16 March 1978 she ran aground on Portsall Rocks. Ultimately she split in three and sank resulting in the largest oil spill of its kind in history to that date; see http://www.c4tx.org/ctx/job/cdb/precis.php5?key=19780316_001 accessed 11 December 2015.
205. Horace B. Robertson (n 87) 865.
206. UNCLOS, Part V, Article 56(1)(b)(iii).
207. Ibid.
208. Ibid.
209. Ibid.
210. Ibid.
211. Ibid.
212. Ibid, Part XII, Sections 1-11, Articles 192-237.
213. Ibid, Part V, Article 56(1)(b)(iii).
214. Ibid, Part XII, Sections 1-11, Articles 192-237.
215. For example, flag State obligations include the duties to adopt pollution control standards in terms of UNCLOS Article 211(2), issue certificates as provided in UNCLOS Article 211(3) and also make periodic inspections as stated in UNCLOS Article 211(3). On the other hand, coastal State obligations include the prohibition of discrimination in terms of UNCLOS Article 227, the prompt release of vessels under UNCLOS Article 226(1)(b) and the observance of the 'recognised rights of the accused' as provided in UNCLOS Article 230(3).
216. Horace B. Robertson (n 87) 865.
217. Ibid.
218. Ibid.
219. Ibid.
220. Ibid, Article 211(5).
221. Ibid.
222. Ibid.
223. Ibid.
224. Horace B. Robertson (n 87) 865.
225. Such information includes for example the port of registry, last port-of-call and next port-of-call; see also UNCLOS, Part XII, Section 6, article 220(3).
226. Horace B. Robertson (n 87) 865.
227. UNCLOS, Part V, Article 56(1)(b)(iii).

228. Horace B. Robertson (n 87) 865.
229. Ibid.
230. When a vessel is voluntarily within a port or at an off-shore terminal of a State, that State may undertake investigations and, where the evidence so warrants, institute proceedings in respect of any discharge from that vessel outside the internal waters, territorial sea or exclusive economic zone of that State in violation of applicable international rules and standards established through the competent international organization or general diplomatic conference; see UNCLOS, Part XII, Section 6, Article 218(1).
231. Subject to section 7, States which, upon request or on their own initiative, have ascertained that a vessel within one of their ports or at one of their off-shore terminals is in violation of applicable international rules and standards relating to seaworthiness of vessels and thereby threatens damage to the marine environment shall, as far as practicable, take administrative measures to prevent the vessel from sailing. Such States may permit the vessel to proceed only to the nearest appropriate repair yard and, upon removal of the causes of the violation, shall permit the vessel to continue immediately; see UNCLOS, Part XII, Section 6, Article 219.
232. Where there are clear grounds for believing that a vessel navigating in the exclusive economic zone or the territorial sea of a State has, in the exclusive economic zone, committed a violation referred to in paragraph 3 resulting in a substantial discharge causing or threatening significant pollution of the marine environment, that State may undertake physical inspection of the vessel for matters relating to the violation if the vessel has refused to give information or if the information supplied by the vessel is manifestly at variance with the evident factual situation and if the circumstances of the case justify such inspection; see UNCLOS, Part XII, Section 6, Article 220(5).
233. Ibid.
234. Where there is clear objective evidence that a vessel navigating in the exclusive economic zone or the territorial sea of a State has, in the exclusive economic zone, committed a violation referred to in paragraph 3 resulting in a discharge causing major damage or threat of major damage to the coastline or related interests of the coastal State, or to any resources of its territorial sea or exclusive economic zone, that State may, subject to section 7, provided that the evidence so warrants, institute proceedings, including detention of the vessel, in accordance with its laws; see UNCLOS, Part XII, Section 6, Article 220(6).
235. Ibid.
236. Horace B. Robertson (n 87) 865.
237. UNCLOS, Part XII, Section 6, Article 220(6).
238. The powers of enforcement against foreign vessels under this Part may only be exercised by officials or by warships, military aircraft, or other ships or aircraft clearly marked and identifiable as being on government service and authorized to that effect; see UNCLOS, Part XII, Section 7, Article 224.
239. UNCLOS, Part XII, Section 7, Article 225.
240. Ibid. Article 226(1)(a).
241. Ibid. Article 226(1)(b).
242. In exercising their rights and performing their duties under this Part, States shall not discriminate in form or in fact against vessels of any other State; see ibid, Article 227.
243. Horace B. Robertson (n 87) 865.
244. UNCLOS, Part XII, Section 7, Article 228(1).
245. Ibid, Article 228(2).
246. Ibid, Article 228(3).
247. Ibid, Article 230(1).
248. Ibid, Article 230(3).
249. Ibid, Article 231.
250. Horace B. Robertson (n 87) 865.
251. Coastal States have the right to adopt and enforce non-discriminatory laws and regulations for the prevention, reduction and control of marine pollution from vessels in ice-covered areas within the limits of the exclusive economic zone, where particularly severe climatic conditions and the presence of ice covering such areas for most of the year create obstructions or exceptional hazards to navigation, and pollution of the marine environment could cause

major harm to or irreversible disturbance of the ecological balance. Such laws and regulations shall have due regard to navigation and the protection and preservation of the marine environment based on the best available scientific evidence; see UNCLOS, Part XII, Section 8, Article 234.

252. Ibid.

253. Ibid.

254. Horace B. Robertson (n 87) 865.

255. UNCLOS, Part XII, Section 8, Article 234.

256. Ibid.

257. Horace B. Robertson (n 87) 865; for example it may be very interesting to consider Article 234 of UNCLOS in an Artic context; see in this sense Janusz Symonides, "Problems and Controversies Concerning Freedom of Navigation in the Arctic" in Lilian del Castillo, *Law of the Sea, From Grotius to the International Tribunal for the Law of the Sea* (Brill Nijhoff, 2015) 227-230.

258. UNCLOS, Part XII, Section 5, Article 211.

259. Ibid, Section 10, Article 236.

260. Ibid, Section 5, Article 211.

261. Ibid, Section 8, Article 234.

262. Ibid, Section 5, Article 211.

263. Ibid, Section 10, Article 236.

264. Ibid.

265. Ibid.

266. Ibid.

267. Ibid.

268. Thomas A. Clingan (n 71) 107-123.

269. UNCLOS, Part XIII, Sections 1-6, Articles 238-365.

270. Thomas A. Clingan (n 71 107-123.

271. UNCLOS, Part XV, Articles 279-299.

272. UNCLOS established what is in effect a two-tier system of judicial settlement is. Part XV of UNCLOS contains the dispute-settlement mechanism in three sections. Section 1 of this Part deals with the settlement of disputes using the traditional public international law procedures founded on the mutual agreement of the parties to the dispute. Part XV Section 2 deals with the procedure in case the parties fail to reach an agreement. Section 3 of Part XV lists exceptions and limitations to the system set out in Section 2; see Thomas Mensah, "The Dispute Settlement Regime of the 1982 United Nations Convention on the Law of the Sea" *Max Planck Yearbook of United Nations Law* (1998) 307-323; see also in general Igor V. Karaman, *Dispute Resolution in the Law of the Sea* (Martinus Nijhoff Publishers, 2012) 1-16.

273. UNCLOS, Part V, Article 56.

274. Horace B. Robertson (n 87) 914-915.

275. Ibid.

276. Ibid.

277. UNCLOS, Part V, Article 56.

278. Ibid.

279. Ibid.

280. Robin Churchill and Alan Vaughn Lowe, *The Law of the Sea* (Manchester University Press, 1988) 133-152.

281. Ibid.

282. UNCLOS, Part V, Article 58.

283. Ibid.

Chapter Two

The Freedom of Overflight in the EEZ

2.1 INTRODUCTION

UNCLOS Article 58 expressly refers to Article 87 of UNCLOS and provides for the high seas freedom of overflight in the EEZ. Its enjoyment is, however, subject to 'the relevant provisions'[1] of UNCLOS and also to the obligation of 'the accommodation of uses'[2] including the express obligation of Article 58(3) of UNCLOS. Generally, the conclusions established above with respect to the high seas freedom of navigation within the EEZ apply *mutatis mutandis* to the freedom of overflight in the EEZ. However, as will be examined below, this freedom poses some important additional limitations.

2.2 PUBLIC INTERNATIONAL AIR LAW

The freedom of overflight is connected to public international air law and is referred to in a number of UNCLOS provisions.[3] It may be argued that public international air law rests on two major principles.[4] The first principle acknowledges the State's absolute sovereignty over the air above its territory and territorial waters.[5] The second principle recognises the air above the high seas as open to all nations and thus not subject to the sovereignty of any State.[6]

Before examining the freedom of overflight the author is to very briefly examine the legal regime applicable to the freedom of the air. Without a proper understanding of the applicable legal regime it may prove difficult to follow the complexities that exist in this context of freedom of overflight. It results that many of the major principles of international law governing airspace[7] are contained in two important treaties i.e. the 1944 Convention on Civil Aviation[8] and UNCLOS. The principle of sovereignty is enunciated in

Articles 1[9] and 2[10] of the Chicago Convention and also in Articles 2[11] and 3[12] of UNCLOS. The principle of sovereignty implies that a State may require any foreign aircraft to comply with its air transport regulations within its airspace. It should be noted, however, that this right is subject to those international treaty obligations the State has assumed in the interest of safe and efficient air transport.[13] Article 37 of the Chicago Convention requires contracting States to:

> collaborate in securing the highest practicable degree of uniformity in regulations, standards, procedures, and organization in relation to aircraft, personnel, airways and auxiliary services in all matters in which such uniformity will facilitate and improve air navigation.[14]

To this end the International Civil Aviation Organisation (ICAO)[15] was granted the explicit power to adopt international standards and recommended practices and procedures.[16] Contracting States may, however, also depart from such practices and standards provided ICAO is notified.[17]

The principle of freedom of overflight is provided for in Articles 87 and 58 of UNCLOS which deal with the freedom of the high seas and the right and duties of other States in the EEZ respectively.[18] Article 12 of the Chicago Convention is based on the freedom of overflight found in international law and it provides that:

> Each contracting State undertakes to adopt measures to insure that every aircraft flying over or maneuvering within its territory and that every aircraft carrying its nationality mark, wherever such aircraft may be, shall comply with the rules and regulations relating to the flight and maneuver of aircraft there in force. Each contracting State undertakes to keep its own regulations in these respects uniform, to the greatest possible extent, with those established from time to time under this Convention. *Over the high seas, the rules in force shall be those established under this Convention.* Each contracting State undertakes to insure the prosecution of all persons violating the regulations applicable.[19]

Contracting States to the Chicago Convention must thus comply with these rules and this to possibly prevent differences in national regulations that might cause navigational hazards to international air transport. Failure to prevent such differences would create obstacles that would 'impede the free passage of aircraft, passengers, crew, baggage, cargo, and mail across international boundaries'.[20] As Buergenthal explains in practice the ICAO Council designates certain rules applicable in the airspace over the high seas as mandatory whilst other rules are not designated as such and thus States may deviate from them.[21]

As happened in the conflict between the United Kingdom and Spain and also in various other conflicts,[22] the freedom of overflight may be greatly restricted due to the establishment of prohibited zones, due to excessive State control over foreign aircraft in transit or even due to national regulations being unreasonably enforced.[23] In the 1967 dispute between the United Kingdom and Spain (UK v Spain), the government of the United Kingdom claimed that Spain established a prohibited zone in the Bay of Algeciraz which prohibited zone according to the United Kingdom would prevent safe landing and take-off to and from the airport of Gibraltar.[24] In this case ICAO's Council gave no decision as at the request of both Spain and the United Kingdom it deferred the disagreement *sine die*.[25] In conflicts like this the freedom of overflight above the high seas becomes very important because it becomes the only means of keeping international air services with a third country.

It has to be noted that State aircraft falls outside the scope of the Chicago Convention. Freedom of overflight to foreign military aircraft is only given in particular situations and therefore the airspace above the high seas is fundamental to those States whose air forces are poised for flight to any part of the world where their interests are challenged.[26] Moore illustrates the importance of freedom of overflight over the high seas by referring to how during the Yom Kippur War the United States had overflight of land territory denied even by its NATO allies.[27]

2.3 FREEDOM OF OVERFLIGHT ABOVE THE HIGH SEAS

It appears that during UNCLOS III air law implications received little attention.[28] However, despite this fact, the provisions of UNCLOS with regards to the freedom of overflight are arguably important. The recognition of the EEZ alone implies restrictions to the traditional freedom of overflight. Before the advent of the EEZ concept and the 'sovereign rights'[29] attached to it, the freedom of overflight was arguably more extensive. It may be argued that when the EEZ came about the freedom of overflight became weaker due to the 'sovereign rights'[30] that coastal States enjoy in the EEZ.

As UNCLOS provides 'no State may validly purport to subject any part of the high seas to its sovereignty'.[31] It follows that the airspace above the high seas is open to aircraft of all States[32] and this limited by the 'peaceful purposes'[33] requirement as was the case with the high seas freedom of navigation.[34] As a general rule it results that coastal States may not control foreign aircraft when in the airspace above the high seas. However, in certain situations provided for in UNCLOS States have 'exceptional and limited jurisdictional enforcement rights'[35] over such foreign aircraft. Article 105[36] is one example where every State has the right to:

> seize a pirate ship or aircraft, or a ship or aircraft taken by piracy and under the control of pirates, and arrest the persons and seize the property on board. The

> courts of the State which carried out the seizure may decide upon the penalties to be imposed, and may also determine the action to be taken with regard to the ships, aircraft or property, subject to the rights of third parties acting in good faith.[37]

Article 87(1)[38] provides that the 'freedom of the high seas…comprises, inter alia, both for coastal and land-locked States the freedom of overflight'.[39] The freedom of overflight as provided for in Article 87(1)(b) of UNCLOS is only one example of the lawful uses of the airspace over the high seas. In fact, freedom of the high seas includes, inter alia, 'use of the ocean airspace for military exercises, aerial reconnaissance, and all other activities of civil and military aircraft if due regard is paid to the rights and interests' of third States.[40] As was the case with the freedom of navigation on the high seas, the freedom of overflight on the high seas is not absolute.[41] As Article 87(1)[42] also provides, the high seas freedom of overflight must also be exercised 'under the conditions laid down by this Convention and by other rules of international law'.[43] Furthermore, Article 87(2)[44] of UNCLOS explicitly subjects the high seas freedom of overflight to the 'due regard'[45] requirement. The 'due regard'[46] obligation is another limitation on the high seas freedom of overflight.[47]

What has already been discussed with respect to the high seas freedom of navigation is applied *mutatis mutandis* to the high seas freedom of overflight.[48]

2.4 FREEDOM OF OVERFLIGHT OVER THE EEZ

As previously discussed, Article 58[49] provides that all States enjoy freedom of overflight in the EEZ, and 'other internationally lawful uses of the sea related to'[50] this freedom is compatible with the provisions of UNCLOS.[51] This freedom in the EEZ is subject to the explicit limitations to which the freedom of navigation is subject to, including Articles 88 to 115 of UNCLOS etc… although it may be argued that many of these articles have no application to aircraft because they specifically deal with ships.[52] For example, this is the case with Article 91 about the 'nationality of ships'.[53] The same may be argued with regards to Articles 92, 93, 94, 95, 96, 97, 98, 99 and 108 which all apply specifically to ships. However, other provisions within Articles 88 to 115, such as Articles 101, 102, 103, 104, 105, 106 and 107, expressly apply to both ships and aircraft and are thus relevant to the freedom of overflight.

It may be argued that Article 58[54] provides for the freedom of overflight in the EEZ to the same extent it provides for the freedom of navigation. This because of the cross-reference to Article 87[55] in Article 58. Article 58[56] additionally contains the requisite that the freedom of overflight's enjoyment is subject to the relevant provisions of UNCLOS and, overall, with the previously mentioned obligation of the accommodation of uses including the previously mentioned obligation of Article 58(3).[57]

It should be noted that what has already been said with respect to the freedom of navigation in the EEZ is applied *mutatis mutandis* to the freedom of overflight in the EEZ. However, UNCLOS is silent on the rights of third States concerning the civil aviation jurisdiction of the coastal State in the airspace above the EEZ.[58] Moreover, UNCLOS is also silent on the applicability of ICAO's aviation code (mandatory to aircraft over the high seas) to aircraft above the EEZ. As such the freedom of overflight in the EEZ poses additional problems when compared to the freedom of navigation in the EEZ. Certain questions may arise in this respect. Does the freedom of overflight include all the activities of the freedom of the high seas, subject to the EEZ provisions? Or is the situation different?[59] Do coastal State enjoy implicit or residual rights that would allow an extension of certain forms of its jurisdiction over the airspace? This may depend on the legal status of the EEZ. If the EEZ is considered as part of the high seas, then naturally freedom of the high seas will prevail and ICAO's aviation code will therefore apply. This may not necessarily be the case if the EEZ is not part of the high seas. An examination of the vast literature on the subject provides no equivocal solutions to the issue. For example, Al Mour observes that the Group of 77[60] has succeeded in establishing a *sui generis* status of the EEZ based *inter alia* on Article 58 of UNCLOS.[61] On the other hand, as Scerni argues the reference to the freedom of the high seas including the freedom of overflight in Article 58(1)[62] and Articles 88 to 115[63] in Article 58(2)[64] amounts to the acceptance of the high seas regime in the EEZ.[65]

From the negotiating context at UNCLOS III it resulted that the legal status of the EEZ was the subject of much disagreement.[66] In this context the author is to make a brief reference to UNCLOS Article 59 always in connection with the freedom of overflight above the EEZ.[67] This article does not specify the legal status of the EEZ nor does it resolve the question of what rights are granted to the coastal State or other States in the EEZ but the word 'equity'[68] contained therein may be taken as a recognition that the legal status of the EEZ must be determined on the basis of an evaluation of the respective rights and interests.[69] The rights and jurisdiction of the coastal State in the airspace above the EEZ and thus including the freedom of overflight above the EEZ must be determined according to the 'purpose for which the question is asked'.[70] It may be argued that with this 'purpose for which the question is asked'[71] the freedom of overflight above the EEZ becomes less ambiguous. In clearer terms the 'purpose for which the question is asked'[72] is the view point of a particular conflict between States as in case of a conflict each State will most probably claim that its UNCLOS rights or jurisdiction are being violated by the other State/s.

The freedoms of UNCLOS Article 58[73] especially the freedom of overflight must not be interpreted very narrowly. As Puri notes the 'sovereign rights'[74] of the coastal State in the EEZ pertain not to the zone itself but to the resources of the zone.[75] As was repeated many times during UNCLOS III, the freedoms under Article 58[76] including the freedom of overflight are qualitatively the same as those of the high seas and as Oxman writes that:

> full freedoms are being preserved, not merely passage rights, and that the application of existing international agreements and regulations regarding navigation, overflight, spacecraft, and submarine cables would be unchanged.[77]

Moreover, the 'sovereign rights'[78] in Article 56(1)[79] imply the exclusive economic use of the EEZ by the coastal State. Thus the 'sovereign rights'[80] of the coastal State incorporates within it the aircraft activities of third States with regard to:

> exploring and exploiting, conserving and managing the natural resources, whether living or non-living, of the waters superjacent to the seabed and of the seabed and its subsoil, and with regard to other activities for the economic exploitation and exploration of the zone, such as the production of energy from the water, currents and winds.[81]

As Hailbronner writes the use of aircraft to explore and exploit fishery resources must as well be regarded as the coastal State's exclusive right.[82]

In addition, it may be argued that the high seas freedom of overflight in the EEZ may be subject to two further possible limitations. Firstly, the coastal State's right to construct artificial islands and structures might prevent low flying in the vicinity of such structures.[83] Secondly, aircraft are subject to the coastal State's competence to regulate the dumping of waste.[84] It may also be argued that the use of the EEZ by foreign military aircraft for the purpose of military exercises is unclear in UNCLOS and thus as Churchill and Lowe state 'there may also be some uncertainty'[85] in this regard. It may be noted that the rules of the air which apply to aircraft in the EEZ are another matter of uncertainty. Under Article 12[86] of the Chicago Convention over the high seas aircraft must comply with the rules of the air laid down by the ICAO.[87] Over a State's territory and territorial sea, however, aircraft must comply with that State's regulations which may diverge from ICAO's rules.[88] In this context, is the EEZ to be regarded as high seas or territorial sea?[89]

2.4.1. Military Overflight (and Navigation)

One of the most controversial issues at UNCLOS III was the military use of the EEZ.[90] However, the subject was only discussed occasionally and was never the object of a formal negotiation.[91] According to Roach and Smith military activities such as 'anchoring, launching and landing of aircraft, operating military devices, intelligence collection, exercises'[92] are recognised 'historic high seas uses preserved by Article 58'[93] of UNCLOS. In terms of UNCLOS Article 58 all States have the right to carry out military activities in the EEZ but this only if consistent with the obligation to have 'due regard'[94] to the rights of the coastal State and other States as specified in UNCLOS. Furthermore, it is the flag State's duty to enforce the 'due regard'[95] obligation.[96] UNCLOS Article 58(1) is intended to facilitate military overflight (and navigation) it guaranteeing 'internationally lawful uses of the seas related to these freedoms...with the operation of ships, aircraft...'.[97] It is also noteworthy that UNCLOS Article 298(1)(b) exempts naval and aerial military disputes from the compulsory dispute settlement mechanism of UNCLOS.[98]

2.4.2. Artificial Islands and Installations

As provided in Article 56(1)(b)[99] of UNCLOS the coastal State has jurisdiction with regard to:

(i) the establishment and use of artificial islands, installations and structures;

(ii) marine scientific research;

(iii) the protection and preservation of the marine environment;[100]

Interestingly enough earlier draft versions used the term 'exclusive jurisdiction'[101] instead of just 'jurisdiction'.[102] In the following paragraphs the author is to comment on the freedom of overflight in connection with Article 56(1)(b)(i), (ii) and (iii).[103]

Article 60[104] is about artificial islands, installations and structures.[105] This article may be seen as very relevant in the context of aircraft flight. From Article 60[106] it is not clear whether the coastal State's jurisdiction reaches the movement by aircraft above, to and from those installations.[107] Article 60(1) of UNCLOS, which will be examined below may be understood to subject all artificial islands to the jurisdiction of the coastal State. However, it appears that this is not the case with all installations and structures. Only the installations and structures specified in Article 60(1)[108] fall within the jurisdiction of the coastal State i.e.:

> (b) installations and structures for the purposes provided for in article 56 and other economic purposes;
>
> (c) installations and structures which may interfere with the exercise of the rights of the coastal State in the zone.[109]

This may imply that installations and structures falling within the said UNCLOS Article 60(1)(b), like for example military installations made for aviation purposes,[110] do not fall within the exclusive jurisdiction of the coastal State. As Gündling explains, proposals to cover all installations were not accepted because a number of States wanted military activities within the EEZ to fall outside the coastal State's control.[111] The installations and structures of article 60(1)(c)[112] fall within the jurisdiction of the coastal State because they 'may interfere'[113] with the rights of the coastal State in the EEZ. UNCLOS Article 60(1)(c), provides no definition of what 'interfere'[114] means and thus as Gündling observes UNCLOS Article 60(1)(c), may give rise to conflicts apart from possibly limiting the freedom of overflight over the EEZ. In the author's opinion Article 60(1)(c)[115] should be interpreted narrowly so as to avoid unnecessary interference with the rights of other States to use the EEZ for purposes other than economic including especially the freedom of overflight. Article 60(1),[116] deals with the regulatory authority in relation to the construction, operation and use of artificial installations and structures. It is not clear whether the regulatory authority of the coastal State includes aircraft movements in the airspace above the EEZ. Moreover, in Part V[117] there is no provision similar to Article 39(3)(a)[118] which regulates 'aircraft in transit'.[119] In terms of UNCLOS Article 39(3)(a) 'aircraft in transit'[120] shall adhere to ICAO's Rules of the Air. Furthermore, UNCLOS Article 39(3)(a) states that State aircraft 'will normally comply with such safety measures and will at all times operate with due regard for the safety of navigation'.[121] The author observes that under Articles 56 and 60 of UNCLOS the regulatory authority of the coastal State is limited to specific matters and it is therefore difficult to incorporate within it the movement of aircraft in the airspace above the EEZ.[122] As Heller writes this problem appears to have escaped the drafters of UNCLOS.[123] He suggests that this problem may have been addressed by an amendment to the then Informal Composite Negotiating Text[124] in order to extend the jurisdiction of the coastal State to aircraft flying in the airspace above the EEZ.[125] To the author's mind Heller's suggestion[126] could have brought uniformity in the rules of the airspace above the territorial sea and EEZ. However, because of the considerable extension in the regulatory authority of the coastal State, restrictions on the freedom of overflight in the EEZ could also have been the result of Heller's suggestion.[127] The author also argues that Heller's suggestion could also have led to inadequate safety standards as ICAO's aviation code could have become superceded by the regulatory authority of the coastal State. For these reasons the author agrees with Hailbronner that ICAO's Rules of the Air should ideally be mandatory in the airspace above the EEZ.[128] It is noteworthy that the coastal State's jurisdiction in the airspace above the EEZ does not include the prescription of operational rules to foreign aircraft as this is not a sovereign economic right.[129]

It may be argued that the situation of aircraft movements to and from artificial installations and structures within the EEZ is different. Firstly, it is not clear if such aircraft movements are covered by Article 60(1).[130] However, to the author's mind the right to construct and use these installations is closely linked to the control of flights to and from these same artificial installations and structures. As Heller states the landing and take-offs at airports established within the EEZ affects the coastal State's rights of control over artificial installations and structures.[131] Furthermore, Walker and Knight note that before the drafting of UNCLOS, discussions took place over whether jurisdiction over activities on artificial installations and structures should be granted to the coastal State, if those activities impact the economic and security interests of the coastal State.[132] It may be argued that landings and take-offs always affect the interests of the coastal State and thus it is reasonable, as Soons comments, to grant the coastal State exclusive aviation jurisdiction over the installations and structures of UNCLOS Article 60(1).[133] The practice of States, as Heller, Lawrence and even Schwenk observe is also in this direction.[134]

Furthermore, Article 60[135] makes no reference to aerial safety zones. However, coastal States may still require aircraft flying above artificial installations and structures to observe the coastal State's regulations regarding these structures.

Artificial islands, installations and structures pose a difficulty[136] and this due to the different 'jurisdictional formulas'[137] found in Article 60(1).[138] This difficulty may in turn limit the freedom of overflight over the EEZ.

2.4.3. Marine Scientific Research

UNCLOS Article 56(1)(b) grants the coastal State jurisdiction 'with regards to marine scientific research'.[139] Article 245[140] *et seq.* deal with marine scientific research. Caflisch and Piccard argue that marine scientific research is usually carried out by ships.[141] However, it may in certain cases also be conducted by aircraft. Article 246(1)[142] grants coastal States the power to regulate, authorize and conduct marine scientific research in their respective EEZ's. In terms of Article 246(2)[143] other States may also conduct marine scientific research in the EEZ of the coastal State but this with the consent of the coastal State. Moreover, Article 246(5)[144] lists a number of exceptions which further put marine scientific research within the coastal State's discretion. The author's opinion is that the freedom of overflight in the EEZ is thus limited by the coastal State's consent. This view is backed by various authors such as Gründling, Caflisch, Piccard and Wolfrüm.[145]

2.4.4. Preservation and Protection of the Marine Environment

UNCLOS Article 56(1)(b) also gives coastal States jurisdiction over the protection and preservation of the marine environment.[146] Article 212[147] deals with marine pollution from civil aircraft and allows States to adopt regulations, laws and measures within its terms.[148] Article 212[149] reflects more or less the Chicago Convention and customary international law.[150] Articles 212[151] and 222[152] exclude coastal State jurisdiction over foreign aircraft in the airspace above the EEZ or high seas with regards to marine pollution and environmental standards.[153] Bearing in mind environmental interests Christol[154] comments negatively on this 'failure'.[155] However, the author argues that an extensive coastal State environmental jurisdiction may seriously limit the freedom of overflight (also the freedom of navigation) in the EEZ. It may be true that foreign aircraft in the EEZ may seriously impact the environmental interests of the coastal State,[156] however, an enlargement of the coastal State's environmental jurisdiction may grant the coastal State wide regulatory powers to the extent that the freedom of overflight (and/or navigation) on the high seas or in the EEZ is severely restricted. The author further argues that what should be required are international environmental standards that effectively apply to aircraft flying over the EEZ and the high seas.

It has to be noted that there are also many claims, not explicitly covered in UNCLOS, to control the airspace over the EEZ (and thus possibly also the airspace above the high seas) related to public order and/or State security.[157] These claims in themselves are threats to the freedom of overflight in the EEZ and/or on the high seas.

2.4.5. Air Defence Identification Zones

An Air Defence Identification Zone (ADIZ) is an area:

> 'in airspace over land or water which may not be over the sovereign territory of a State in which ready identification, location and control of all aircraft is required in the interest of national security'.[158]

The main reason to establish an ADIZ is, according to Petras, 'to properly identify all approaching aircraft for security purposes so that they could, prior to entry into national airspace, satisfy certain local entry requirements'.[159] In other words ADIZs give the State more chance to respond to possibly hostile aircraft.[160] Furthermore, no definition of an ADIZ is found in international conventions and ADIZs are not regulated by an international authority.[161]

According to Hailbronner, the establishment of ADIZs is a major claim to aerial jurisdiction.[162] As various authors observe ADIZs have usually been justified by the doctrine of necessity or by analogy to the contiguous zone concept.[163] It may be argued that ADIZs are fundamental to prevent 'surprise attacks or infringements upon essential security interests and to ensure the safety of international air traffic'.[164] However, the author argues that ADIZs may limit the freedom of overflight in the EEZ. The requisite of identification alone may not interfere with the freedom of overflight in the EEZ, however, interference with the movement of aircraft in these ADIZs may restrict the freedom of overflight even on the high seas. It is noteworthy that UNCLOS grants no aerial defence rights or jurisdiction to coastal States. In fact, military security and defence are only briefly mentioned in Article 39.[165]

ADIZs are different from the 'temporary exclusive use'[166] of specific high seas areas. This 'temporary exclusive'[167] military use is generally accepted as McDougal and Burke assert.[168] However, this is only a 'temporary'[169] limitation on the freedom of overflight. Restrictions on the freedom of overflight are only justified if not on a permanent basis and as Hailbronner[170] writes never accepted if not 'temporary'.[171] A case in point are the protests of several States against the former French ADIZs off the coast of Algeria.[172]

2.4.6. Hot Pursuit of Aircraft

Some authors like Poulantzas and McDougal refer to what they call 'hot pursuit of aircraft'.[173] This 'hot pursuit of aircraft'[174] is mainly an extended analogy of the hot pursuit of ships comprehensively found in Article 111.[175] The doctrine of hot pursuit of ships[176] recognises the coastal State's right to pursue a foreign vessel, that violated its laws while within its waters, on the high seas.[177] Gamboa argues that a State has a right to:

> pursue onto the high seas and arrest a foreign vessel which has committed an offence within its waters. The hot pursuit has to commence when the offending vessel is within the national waters, territorial sea or contiguous zone of the pursuing state and must come to an end when the vessel has entered part of its own country or of a third state. The pursuit must be uninterrupted and only necessary and reasonable force may be used to effect the seizure and bringing into port of the pursuit ship.[178]

UNCLOS Article 111 gives coastal States the right to pursue and arrest vessels on the high seas provided that:

> 1. The pursuers are the 'competent authorities'[179] of the coastal State;
> 2. The 'competent authorities'[180] of the coastal State have 'good reason to believe'[181] that the pursued vessel violated the coastal State's 'laws and regulations';[182]
> 3. The pursuit starts when the pursuing vessel is in the coastal State's 'internal waters, the archipelagic waters, the territorial sea or the contiguous zone';[183]
> 4. The pursuit is continuous.

Authors like Hailbronner[184] oppose this 'hot pursuit of aircraft'[185] stating that State practice does not support this view.[186] According to Hailbronner State practice, as reflected in national laws, usually only refers to hot pursuit of ships.[187] 'Hot pursuit of aircraft',[188] if recognised at all by States, may further limit the freedom of overflight in the EEZ and/or even on the high seas.

2.5 CONCLUSION

In conclusion, the 'sovereign rights'[189] of the coastal State in the EEZ affected the traditional high seas freedom of overflight in the EEZ to the extent that it arguably suffered restrictions. In the author's opinion many of the limitations existent in the context of the freedom of overflight in the EEZ are shared with the high seas freedom of navigation in the EEZ.[190] Furthermore, UNCLOS does not always provide straightforward answers to specific questions like for example issues relating to the legal status of the EEZ which may in turn affect the freedom of overflight in the EEZ.[191] In the author's opinion a balance between the rights of the coastal State and the freedom of overflight in the EEZ has to be achieved. To the author's mind such a balance may generally result by interpreting UNCLOS provisions in favour of the traditional freedom of overflight as a principle of customary international law.[192]

NOTES

1. UNCLOS, Part V, Article 58.
2. See for a detailed explanation Francisco Orrego Vicuña, *The Exclusive Economic Zone, Regime and Legal Nature under International Law* (Cambridge University Press, 1989) 93-103.
3. For example, UNCLOS Articles 36, 38, 44, 53, 58, 87 and 297 make express reference to the freedom of overflight.
4. Kay Hailbronner, "Freedom of the Air and the Convention on the Law of the Sea" *The American Journal of International Law* 77 (1983) 490.
5. 2(1) The sovereignty of a coastal State extends, beyond its land territory and internal waters and, in the case of an archipelagic State, its archipelagic waters, to an adjacent belt of sea, described as the territorial sea.

(2) *This sovereignty extends to the air space over the territorial sea as well as to its bed and subsoil.*

(3) The sovereignty over the territorial sea is exercised subject to this Convention and to other rules of international law; see UNCLOS, Part II, Section 1, Article 2.

6. Ibid, Part VII, Section 1, Article 89; see also Michael Milde, *International Air Law and ICAO* (Eleven International Publishing, 2008) 33-57.
7. That is the two major principles highlighted above.
8. Convention on International Civil Aviation (adopted 7 December 1944, entered into force 4 April 1947) 15 UNTS 295, hereinafter referred to as the Chicago Convention; see in general for the relationship between the Chicago Convention and the EEZ Jean-Louis Magdelé-

nat, "Les Implications de la Nouvelle Convention sur le Droit de la Mere en Droit Aérien" *Annuaire de Droit Maritime et Aérien* 8 (1985) 323-338.

9. The contracting States recognize that every State has complete and exclusive sovereignty over the airspace above its territory.

10. For the purposes of this Convention the territory of a State shall be deemed to be the land areas and territorial waters adjacent thereto under the sovereignty, suzerainty, protection or mandate of such State.

11. 1. The sovereignty of a coastal State extends, beyond its land territory and internal waters and, in the case of an archipelagic State, its archipelagic waters, to an adjacent belt of sea, described as the territorial sea.

2. This sovereignty extends to the air space over the territorial sea as well as to its bed and subsoil.

3. The sovereignty over the territorial sea is exercised subject to this Convention and to other rules of international law.

12. Every State has the right to establish the breadth of its territorial sea up to a limit not exceeding 12 nautical miles, measured from baselines determined in accordance with this Convention.

13. Kay Hailbronner (n 4) 490-519; see also in general Michael Milde, "United Nations Convention on the Law of the Sea – Possible Implications for International Air Law" *Annals of Air and Space Law* 8 (1983) 167-201.

14. Chicago Convention, Part 1, Chapter 6, Article 37; see also comments on Article 37 Ruwantissa Abeyratne, *Convention on International Civil Aviation: A Commentary* (Springer International Publishing, 2014).

15. ICAO is a UN specialised agency which was founded by States in 1994 to 'manage the administration and governance' of the Chicago Convention. ICAO works with State Parties to 'reach consensus on international civil aviation Standards and Recommended Practices (SARPs) and policies in support of a safe, efficient, secure, economically sustainable and environmentally responsible civil aviation sector'. Furthermore, ICAO also 'coordinates assistance and capacity building for States in support of numerous aviation development objectives; produces global plans to coordinate multilateral strategic progress for safety and air navigation; monitors and reports on numerous air transport sector performance metrics; and audits States' civil aviation oversight capabilities in the areas of safety and security'; see http://www.icao.int/about-icao/Pages/default.aspx accessed 5 February 2016; see also in general ICAO, *ICAO: The Story of the International Civil Aviation Organization* (Public Information Office of ICAO, 1969); see also in general David Mackenzie, *ICAO: A History of the International Civil Aviation Organization* (University of Toronto Press, 2010).

16. See in general Thomas Buergenthal, *Law Making in the International Civil Aviation Organisation* (University of Virginia Press, 1969); see also Jochen Erler, *Rechtsfragen der ICAO* (Heymann, 1967) 131; see also Nicolas Matte, *Traité de droit aérien-aéronautique : évolution, problèmes spatiaux* (Éditions A. Pedone, 1964) 195-197; see also Michael Milde (n 6) 119-193.

17. Ibid.

18. It is also recognised in article 2 of the 1958 HSC.

19. Chicago Convention, Part 1, Chapter 2, Article 12; see also comments on Article 12 Ruwantissa Abeyratne (n 14).

20. See http://www.nationsencyclopedia.com/United-Nations-Related-Agencies/The-International-Civil-Aviation-Organization-ICAO-ACTIVITIES.html accessed 5 February 2016.

21. Thomas Buergenthal (n 16) 57; it is interesting to note that, as various authors observe, the Chicago Conference failed to establish a multilateral treaty regime providing for freedoms of overflight and landing and thus the granting of traffic rights continued to fall within the sovereign powers of each State; see Nicolas Matte (n 16) 241; see also Johnson, *Rights in Airspace* (Manchester University Press, 1965) 58; see also Oliver Lissitzyn, "Freedom of the Air: Scheduled and Non-Scheduled Air Services" in McWhinney and Bradley, *The Freedom of the Air* (McGill University, 1965) 89; see the ICAO Rules of the Air for mandatory and non-mandatory rules.

22. Other examples of conflicts include disputes between Turkey and Greece, the Arab States and Israel on the establishment of prohibited zones; see Nicolas Matte (n 16) 241 for a similar 1971 dispute between India and Pakistan (Pakistan v India); see also Jochen Erler (n 16) 192; see also Michael Milde (n 6) 189.
23. Kay Hailbronner (n 4) 490-494.
24. See Michael Milde (n 6) 189.
25. Ibid.
26. Kay Hailbronner (n 4) 490-494.
27. John Norton Moore, "The Regime of Straits and the Third United Nations Conference on the Law of the Sea" *American Journal of International Law* 74 (1980) 84; see also O'Connell, "Innocent Passage of Warships" *Thesaurus Acroasium* 7 (1977) 446-447; see also Pradelle Paul, "Les frontières de l'air" Recueil Des Cours 86 (1954) 139.
28. Kay Hailbronner (n 4) 490-494.
29. UNCLOS, Part V, Article 56.
30. Ibid.
31. UNCLOS, Part VII, Section 1, Article 89.
32. Ibid, Article 87(1).
33. Ibid, Article 88.
34. See Chapter 1, Sections 1.3.2. and 1.4.1.3.
35. J.C. Cooper, *The Right to Fly* (New York, 1947) 126; see also M. McDougal and W. Burke, *The Public Order of the Oceans: A Contemporary International Law of the Sea* (Martinus Nijhoff Publishers, 1987) 782-794.
36. UNCLOS, Part VII, Section 1, Article 105.
37. Ibid.
38. Ibid, Article 87(1).
39. Ibid.
40. Kay Hailbronner (n 4) 490-519.
41. See Chapter 1, Section 1.3.
42. UNCLOS, Part VII, Section 1, Article 87(1).
43. Ibid; see Chapter 1, Section 1.3 which is fully applicable to the high seas freedom of overflight.
44. Ibid, Article 87(2).
45. Ibid.
46. Ibid.
47. See Chapter 1, Section 1.3.1.
48. See Chapter 1, Section 1.3.
49. UNCLOS, Part V, Article 58.
50. Ibid.
51. Ibid.
52. Robin Churchill and Alan Vaughn Lowe, *The Law of the Sea* (Manchester University Press, 1988) 133-152.
53. UNCLOS, Part VII, Section 1, Article 91.
54. Ibid, Part V, Article 58.
55. Ibid, Part VII, Section 1, Article 87.
56. Ibid.
57. Ibid, Part V, Article 58(3).
58. Kay Hailbronner (n 4) 490-519.
59. Francisco Orrega Vicuña (n 2) 93-120.
60. The Group of 77 was established by seventy-seven developing countries on 15 June 1964, which seventy-seven developing countries were signatories of the 'Joint Declaration of the Seventy-Seven Developing Countries'. The Group of 77 is considered as 'the largest intergovernmental organization of developing countries in the United Nations which provides the means for the countries of the South to articulate and promote their collective economic interests and enhance their joint negotiating capacity on all major international economic issues within the United Nations system, and promote South-South cooperation for development'; see

http://www.g77.org/doc/ accessed 5 February 2016; see also in general Karl Sauvant, *The Group of 77: Evolution, Structure, Organization* (Oceana Publications, 1981).

61. Awadh Mohamed Al Mour, "The Legal Status of the Exclusive Economic Zone" *Revue Egyptienne de Droit International* 33 (1977) 60; see on the legal status of the EEZ Bárbara Kwiatkowska, *The 200 [Two Hundred] Mile Exclusive Economic Zone in the New Law of the Sea* (Martinus Nijhoff Publishers, 1989) 230; see also James Wang, *Handbook on Ocean Politics and Law* (Greenwood Publishing Group, 1992) 69; see also Lewis Alexander and Robert Hodgson, "The Impact of the 200-Mile Economic Zone on the Law of the Sea" *San Diego Law Review* 12 (1975) 569-599; see also Calixto Armas Barea and Frida Pfirter de Armas, "Consideraciones Sobre la Naturaleza Jurídica la Zona Económica Exclusiva" *Anuario Argentino de Derecho Internactional* (1983) 37-53; see also P.D. Oelofsen, "Some Observations on the Concept of the Exclusive Economic Zone" South African Yearbook of International Law 1 (1975) 46-62.

62. UNCLOS, Part V, Article 58(1).

63. Ibid, Part VII, Section 1, Articles 88 to 115.

64. Ibid, Part V, Article 58(2).

65. Mario Scerni, "La Zone Économique Exclusive: Son Importance, sa Nature Juridique et les Problèmes Principaux Relatifs" in *Thesaurus Acroasium of the Institute of Public International Law and International Relations of Thessaloniki: Volume VII* (Thessaloniki Institute of Public International Law and International Relations, 1977) 157.

66. E.D. Brown, "The Exclusive Economic Zone: Criteria and Machinery for the Resolution of International Conflicts between Different Users of the EEZ" *Maritime Policy and Management* 4 (1977) 325-250; see also Günther Jaenicke, "Die Dritte Seerechtskonferenz der Vereinten Nationen" *Zeitschrift für Ausländisches Recht und Völkerrecht* 38 (1978) 489.

67. UNCLOS, Part V, Article 59.

68. Ibid.

69. Kay Hailbronner (n 4) 490-519.

70. Heller, 'Air Space over Extended Jurisdictional Zones' in J.K. Gamble, *Law of the Sea: Neglected Issues* (University of Hawaii, 1979) 135; see also Bernard H. Oxman, "The Third United Nations Conference on the Law of the Sea: the 1976 New York Session" *American Journal of International Law* 72 (1977) 260-261.

71. Ibid.

72. Ibid.

73. UNCLOS, Part V, Article 58.

74. Ibid.

75. Rama Puri, "Evolution of the Concept of the Exclusive Economic Zone in UNCLOS III: India's Contribution" *Journal of the Indian Law Institute* 22 (1980) 509.

76. UNCLOS, Part V, Article 58.

77. Bernard H. Oxman, "An Analysis of the Exclusive Economic Zone as formulated in the Informal Composite Negotiating Text" in Thomas A. Clingan, *Law of the Sea: State Practice in Zones of Special Jurisdiction* (Honolulu Law of the Sea Institute, 1982) 69; see also Thomas Clingan, "Emerging Law of the Sea: The Economic Zone Dilemma" San Diego Law Review 14 (1977) 530-547.

78. UNCLOS, Part V, Article 56.

79. Ibid, Article 56(1).

80. Ibid.

81. Ibid.

82. Kay Hailbronner (n 4) 490-519.

83. Ibid; see also Section 2.3.1. below.

84. Ibid.

85. Ibid; see Section 2.3.4. below.

86. Chicago Convention, Part 1, Chapter 2, Article 12.

87. Robin Churchill and Alan Vaughn Lowe (n 52) 133-152.

88. Ibid; Any State which finds it impracticable to comply in all respects with any such international standards or procedure, or to bring its own regulations or practices into full accord with any international standard or procedure after amendment of the latter, or which deems it

necessary to adopt regulations or practices differing in any particular respect from those established by an international standard, shall give immediate notification to the International Civil Aviation Organization of the differences between its own practice and that established by the international standard. In the case of amendments to international standards, any State which does not make the appropriate amendments to its own regulations or practices shall give notice to the Council within sixty days of the adoption of the amendment to the international standard, or indicate the action which it proposes to take. In any such case, the Council shall make immediate notification to all other States of the difference which exists between one or more features of an international standard and the corresponding national practice of that State; see Chicago Convention, Part 1, Chapter 6, Article 38.

89. Robin Churchill and Alan Vaughn Lowe (n 52) 133-152.

90. Francisco Orrego Vicuña (n 2) 103-120; see on the military uses of the sea in general R.W.G. de Muralt, "The Military Aspects of the U.N. Law of the Sea Convention" *Netherlands International Law Review* 32 (1985) 78-99; see also Michael Morris, "Military Aspects of the Exclusive Economic Zone" *Ocean Yearbook* 3 (1982) 320-348; see also Scott Truver, "The Law of the Sea and the Military Use of the Oceans in 2010" *Louisiana Law Review* 45 (1984) 1221-1247; see also David Larson, "Security Issues and the Law of the Sea: a General Framework" *Ocean Development and International Law* 15 (1985) 99-146; see also Elmar Rauch, "Military Uses of the Oceans" *German Yearbook of International Law* 28 (1985) 229-267; see also Francesco Francioni, "Peacetime Use of Force, Military Activities, and the New Law of the Sea" *Cornell International Law Journal* 18 (1985) 203-226.

91. See ibid; see also Reynaldo Pohl, "The Exclusive Economic Zone in the Light of Negotiations of the Third United Nations Conference on the Law of the Sea" in Francesco Orrego Vicuña, *The Exclusive Economic Zone: a Latin American Perspective* (Westview Press, 1984) 54-55; see also Alfonso Schreiber, "The Exclusive Economic Zone: its Legal Nature and the Problem of Military Uses" in Francesco Orrego Vicuña, *The Exclusive Economic Zone: a Latin American Perspective* (Westview Press, 1984) 139-140.

92. J. Ashley Roach and Robert Smith, *United States Responses to Excessive Maritime Claims* (Springer Netherlands, 1996) 407-423.

93. Ibid.

94. UNCLOS, Part V, Article 58.

95. Ibid.

96. J. Ashley Roach and Robert Smith (n 92) 407-423.

97. UNCLOS, Part V, Article 58(1); see also David Joseph Attard, *The Exclusive Economic Zone in International Law* (Clarendon Press, 1987) 84-86.

98. David Joseph Attard (n 97) 84-86.

99. Ibid, Article 56(1)(b).

100. Ibid; see in general Nikos Papadakis, *The International Legal Regime of Artificial Islands* (Sijthoff Publications, 1977).

101. Lothar Gündling, "Die Exclusive Wirtschaftszone" *Zeitschrift für Ausländisches Öffentliches Recht* 38 (1978) 627.

102. UNCLOS, Part V, Article 56(1)(b).

103. Ibid, Article 56(1)(b)(i),(ii) and (iii).

104. Ibid, Article 60.

105. See in general Fritz Münch, "Les Iles Artificielles et les Installations en Mer" *Zeitschrift für Ausländisches Öffentliches Recht* 38 (1978) 933-958.

106. UNCLOS, Part V, Article 60.

107. Kay Hailbronner (n 4) 490-518.

108. UNCLOS, Part V, Article 60(1).

109. Ibid, Article 60(1)(b) and (c).

110. See Günther Jaenicke (n 66) 487.

111. Lothar Gündling (n 101) 640.

112. UNCLOS, Part V, Article 60(1)(c).

113. Ibid.

114. Ibid.

115. Ibid.

116. Ibid, Article 60(1).
117. Ibid, Articles 55-75.
118. Ibid, Part III, Section 2, Article 39(3)(a).
119. Ibid.
120. Ibid.
121. Ibid.
122. Kay Hailbronner (n 4) 503-510.
123. Heller (n 70) 135-153.
124. The Third Session of UNCLOS took place in Geneva between 26 March 1975 and 10 May 1975. On 18 April 1975 the Conference requested the Chairman of each Main Committee to prepare a Single Negotiating Text about the subjects given to his/her respective Committee. Three separate texts resulted and together they were called the 'Informal Single Negotiating Text' (SNT) around which the further discussions at UNCLOS revolved. In July 1975 the President prepared another Single Negotiating Text on dispute settlement. In May 1976 the popular Revised Single Negotiating Text (RSNT) was prepared. In July 1977 the four separate texts were put together into one 'Informal Composite Negotiating Text'; see *Informal Composite Negotiating Text* (Office of Law of the Sea Negotiations, Department of State 1977); see also S.P. Jagota, *Maritime Boundary* (Martinus Nijhoff Publishers, 1985) 223-227.
125. Ibid.
126. Ibid.
127. Ibid.
128. Kay Hailbronner (n 4) 503-510.
129. Ibid.
130. UNCLOS, Part V, Article 60.
131. Heller (n 70) 135-153.
132. Craig Walker, "Jurisdictional Problems Created by Artificial Islands" *San Diego Law Review* 10 (1973) 662; see also Gary Knight, "International Legal Aspects of Deep Draft Harbour Facilities" *Journal of Maritime Law and Commerce* 4 (1973) 386.
133. Alfred Soons, *Artificial Islands and Installations in International Law* (Law of the Sea Institute - University of Rhode Island, 1974) 1-30.
134. Heller (n 70) 150; see also Walter Schwenk, "Die Anwendung luftrechtlicher Vorschriften bei Flügen von und nach Schiffen und Bohrinseln" *Zeitschrift für Luft- und Weltraumrecht* (1976) 234; see also William H. Lawrence, "Superports, Airports and Other Fixed Installations on the High Seas" Journal of Maritime Law and Commerce 6 (1975) 575-591.
135. UNCLOS, Part V, Article 60.
136. Francisco Orrega Vicuña (n 2) 93-120.
137. Ibid.
138. UNCLOS, Part V, Article 60(1).
139. Ibid; see in general Florian Th Wegelein, *Marine Scientific Research: The Operation and Status of Research Vessels and Other Platforms in International Law* (Martinus Nijhoff Publishers, 2005); for more information see in general Judith Fenwick, *International Profiles on Marine Scientific Research: National Maritime Claims, MSR Jurisdiction, and U.S. Research Clearance Histories for the World's Coastal States* (Woods Hole Oceanographic Institution, 1992); see also in general Tim Stephens and Donald Rothwell, "Marine Scientific Research" in Donald Rothwell, Alex Oude Elferink, Karen Scott and Tim Stephens, *The Oxford Handbook of the Law of the Sea* (Oxford University Press, 2015) 559.
140. Ibid, Part XIII, Section 3, Article 245.
141. Caflisch and Piccard, "The Legal Regime of Marine Scientific Research and the Third United Nations Conference on the Law of the Sea" *Zeitschrift für ausländisches öffentliches Recht* (1978) 848.
142. UNCLOS, Part XIII, Section 3, Article 246(1).
143. Ibid, Article 246(2).
144. Ibid, Article 246(5).
145. Caflisch and Piccard (n 141) 873; see also Gündling (n 101) 642; see also Wolfrum, "Der Schutz der Meeresforschung in Völkerrecht" *German Year Book of International Law* (1976) 99.

146. See in general Robin Churchill, "The LOSC Regime for Protection of the Marine Environment – Fit for the Twenty-First Century?" in Rosemary Rayfuse, *Research Handbook on International Marine Environmental Law* (Edward Elgar Publishing Ltd, 2015) 3-30; see also Yoshifumi Tanaka, "Principles of International Marine Environmental Law" in Rosemary Rayfuse, *Research Handbook on International Marine Environmental Law* (Edward Elgar Publishing Ltd, 2015) 31-56; see also James Harrison, "Actors and Institutions for the Protection of the Marine Environment" in Rosemary Rayfuse, *Research Handbook on International Marine Environmental Law* (Edward Elgar Publishing Ltd, 2015) 57-78; see also Kiss, "La Pollution du milieu marin" *Zeitschrift für ausländisches öffentliches Recht* (1978) 902.

147. UNCLOS, Part XII, Section 5, Article 212.

148. (2) States shall take other measures as may be necessary to prevent, reduce and control such pollution.

(3) States, acting especially through competent international organizations or diplomatic conference, shall endeavour to establish global and regional rules, standards and recommended practices and procedures to prevent, reduce and control such pollution; see Ibid, Article 212(2) and (3).

149. Ibid, Article 212.

150. Kay Hailbronner (n 4) 510-513.

151. Ibid.

152. States shall enforce, within the air space under their sovereignty or with regard to vessels flying their flag or vessels or aircraft of their registry, their laws and regulations adopted in accordance with article 212, paragraph 1, and with other provisions of this Convention and shall adopt laws and regulations and take other measures necessary to implement applicable international rules and standards established through competent international organizations or diplomatic conference to prevent, reduce and control pollution of the marine environment from or through the atmosphere, in conformity with all relevant international rules and standards concerning the safety of air navigation; see Ibid, Part XIII, Section 6, Article 222.

153. Kay Hailbronner (n 4) 510-513.

154. Christol, "Unilateral Claims for the Use of Ocean Airspace" in J.K. Gamble, *Law of the Sea: Neglected Issues* (University of Hawaii, 1979) 130.

155. Ibid.

156. M. McDougal and W. Burke (n 35) 848; see also M. McDougal, H. Lasswell and I. Vlasic, *Public Order in Space* (Yale University Press, 1964) 308; see also Roberts, "The State of the Art in Weather Modification" in H.J. Taubenfeld, *Weather Modification and the Law* (Oceana Publications, 1968) 20; see also Christol, "Aircraft and the International Legal and Institutional Aspects of the Stratospheric Ozone Problem" *Annals of Air and Space Law* (1976) 3.

157. M. McDougal and W. Burke (n 35) 782; see also M. McDougal, H. Lasswell and I. Vlasic (n 156) 306.

158. Ruwantissa Abeyratne, "In Search of Theoretical Justification for Air Defense Identification Zones" *Journal of Transportation Security* 5 (2012) 87; see also Andrew Williams, "The Interception of Civil Aircraft over the High Seas in the Global War on Terror" *Air Force Law Review* 73 (2007) 95-96l; see also Ruwantissa Abeyratne, *Air Navigation Law* (Springer International Publishing, 2012) 11-16.

159. Christopher Petras, "The Law of Air Mobility: the International Legal Principles behind the U.S. Mobility Air Forces' Mission." *Air Force Law Review* 66 (2010) 62-63; see also Peter Dutton, "*Caelium Liberum:* Air Defence Identification Zones Outside Sovereign Airspace" *American Journal of International Law* 103 (2009) 691; see also Mark Franklin, "Sovereignty and Functional Airspace Blocks" *Air Space Law* 32 (2007) 425.

160. Jeremy Page, 'The A to Z on China's Air Defense Identification Zone' *The Wall Street Journal* (27 November 2013); see http://blogs.wsj.com/chinarealtime/2013/11/27/the-a-to-z-on-chinas-air-defense-identification-zone/ accessed 5 February, 2016.

161. Ibid.

162. Kay Hailbronner (n 4) 490.

163. M. McDougal, H. Lasswell and I. Vlasic (n 156) 306; see also Robert Hayton, *Jurisdiction of the Littoral State in the "Air Frontier"* (Philippine Society of International Law, 1964)

369; see also Georgiades, "Du Nationalisme Aerien a l'Internationalisme Spatial ou le Mythe de la Souverainete Aerienne" *Revue Française de Droit Aérien Spatial* (1962) 129; see also J. Murchison, *The Contiguous Air Space Zone in International Law* (Department of National Defence (Ottawa), 1957) 1; see also Head, "ADIZ, International Law and Contiguous Airspace" *Alberta Law Review* (1964) 182; see in general on the contiguous zone Shigeru Oda, "The Concept of the Contiguous Zone" *International and Comparative Law Quarterly* 11 (1962) 131-153; see also Sir Gerald Fitzmaurice, "Some Results of the Geneva Conference on the Law of the Sea" *International and Comparative Law Quarterly* 8 (1959) 73-121; see also Gilbert Gidel, "La Mer Territoriale et la Zone Contiguë" *Collected Courses of the Hague Academy of International Law* 48 (1934) 241-273; see also Silvina Bakardzhieva, *The Delimitation of the Contiguous Zone – Implementation of Article 33 of 1983 UNCLOS into Bulgarian Legislation* (Silvina Bakardzhieva, 2015).

164. Christol (n 154) 128.

165. 1. Ships and aircraft, while exercising the right of transit passage, shall:

(a) proceed without delay through or over the strait;

(b) refrain from any threat or use of force against the sovereignty, territorial integrity or political independence of States bordering the strait, or in any other manner in violation of the principles of international law embodied in the Charter of the United Nations;

(c) refrain from any activities other than those incident to their normal modes of continuous and expeditious transit unless rendered necessary by force majeure or by distress;

(d) comply with other relevant provisions of this Part.

2. Ships in transit passage shall:

(a) comply with generally accepted international regulations, procedures and practices for safety at sea, including the International Regulations for Preventing Collisions at Sea;

(b) comply with generally accepted international regulations, procedures and practices for the prevention, reduction and control of pollution from ships.

3. Aircraft in transit passage shall:

(a) observe the Rules of the Air established by the International Civil Aviation Organization as they apply to civil aircraft; state aircraft will normally comply with such safety measures and will at all times operate with due regard for the safety of navigation;

(b) at all times monitor the radio frequency assigned by the competent internationally designated air traffic control authority or the appropriate international distress radio frequency; see UNCLOS, Part III, Section 2, Article 39.

166. M. McDougal, H. Lasswell and I. Vlasic (n 156) 303; see also M. McDougal and W. Burke (n 35) 787; see also McDougal and Schlei, "The Hydrogen Bomb Tests in Perspective: Lawful Measures for Security" The Yale Law Journal (1955) 648.

167. Ibid.

168. M. McDougal and W. Burke (n 35) 594 *et seq.*; see also M. McDougal, H. Lasswell and I. Vlasic (n 156) 310.

169. M. McDougal, H. Lasswell and I. Vlasic (n 156) 303; see also M. McDougal and W. Burke (n 35) 787; see also McDougal and Schlei (n 166) 648.

170. Kay Hailbronner (n 4) 515-519.

171. M. McDougal, H. Lasswell and I. Vlasic (n 156) 303; see also M. McDougal and W. Burke (n 35) 787; see also McDougal and Schlei (n 166) 648.

172. Kay Hailbronner, *Der Schutz der Luftgrenzen im Frieden* (Heymann, 1972) 81-87.

173. M. McDougal, H. Lasswell and I. Vlasic (n 156) 310; see also N. Poulantzas, *The Right of Hot Pursuit in International Law* (Martinus Nijhoff Publishers, 2002) 298.

174. Ibid.

175. 1. The hot pursuit of a foreign ship may be undertaken when the competent authorities of the coastal State have good reason to believe that the ship has violated the laws and regulations of that State. Such pursuit must be commenced when the foreign ship or one of its boats is within the internal waters, the archipelagic waters, the territorial sea or the contiguous zone of the pursuing State, and may only be continued outside the territorial sea or the contiguous zone if the pursuit has not been interrupted. It is not necessary that, at the time when the foreign ship within the territorial sea or the contiguous zone receives the order to stop, the ship giving the order should likewise be within the territorial sea or the contiguous zone. If the foreign ship is

within a contiguous zone, as defined in Article 33, the pursuit may only be undertaken if there has been a violation of the rights for the protection of which the zone was established.

2. The right of hot pursuit shall apply mutatis mutandis to violations in the exclusive economic zone or on the continental shelf, including safety zones around continental shelf installations, of the laws and regulations of the coastal State applicable in accordance with this Convention to the exclusive economic zone or the continental shelf, including such safety zones.

3. The right of hot pursuit ceases as soon as the ship pursued enters the territorial sea of its own State or of a third State.

4. Hot pursuit is not deemed to have begun unless the pursuing ship has satisfied itself by such practicable means as may be available that the ship pursued or one of its boats or other craft working as a team and using the ship pursued as a mother ship is within the limits of the territorial sea, or, as the case may be, within the contiguous zone or the exclusive economic zone or above the continental shelf. The pursuit may only be commenced after a visual or auditory signal to stop has been given at a distance which enables it to be seen or heard by the foreign ship.

5. The right of hot pursuit may be exercised only by warships or military aircraft, or other ships or aircraft clearly marked and identifiable as being on government service and authorized to that effect.

6. Where hot pursuit is effected by an aircraft:

(a) the provisions of paragraphs 1 to 4 shall apply mutatis mutandis;

(b) the aircraft giving the order to stop must itself actively pursue the ship until a ship or another aircraft of the coastal State, summoned by the aircraft, arrives to take over the pursuit, unless the aircraft is itself able to arrest the ship. It does not suffice to justify an arrest outside the territorial sea that the ship was merely sighted by the aircraft as an offender or suspected offender, if it was not both ordered to stop and pursued by the aircraft itself or other aircraft or ships which continue the pursuit without interruption.

7. The release of a ship arrested within the jurisdiction of a State and escorted to a port of that State for the purposes of an inquiry before the competent authorities may not be claimed solely on the ground that the ship, in the course of its voyage, was escorted across a portion of the exclusive economic zone or the high seas, if the circumstances rendered this necessary.

8. Where a ship has been stopped or arrested outside the territorial sea in circumstances which do not justify the exercise of the right of hot pursuit, it shall be compensated for any loss or damage that may have been thereby sustained; see UNCLOS, Part VII, Section 1, Article 111.

176. Interesting to compare with the right of hot pursuit under the 1958 HSC; see Nickolaos Poulantzas, "The Right of Hot Pursuit Especially Under the Geneva Convention on the High Seas" *Revue Hellénique de Droit International* 14 (1961) 198-224.

177. Allen Craig, "Doctrine of Hot Pursuit: A Functional Interpretation Adaptable to Emerging Maritime Law Enforcement Technologies and Practices" *Ocean Development and International Law* 20 (1989) 309.

178. Melquiades Gamboa, *A Dictionary of International Law and Diplomacy* (Phoenix Press, 1973) 139-140. Gamboa's definition of the doctrine of hot pursuit of ships more or less reiterates Article 23(1) of the 1958 HSC; see in general Nicholas Poúlantzas, *The Right of Hot Pursuit in International Law* (Martinus Nijhoff Publishers, 2002).

179. UNCLOS, Part VII, Section 1, Article 111.

180. Ibid.

181. Ibid.

182. Ibid.

183. Ibid.

184. Kay Hailbronner (n 4) 519.

185. M. McDougal, H. Lasswell and I. Vlasic (n 156) 310; see also N. Poulantzas (n 526) 173.

186. Kay Hailbronner (n 172) 81-87.

187. Ibid.

188. M. McDougal, H. Lasswell and I. Vlasic (n 156) 310; see also N. Poulantzas (n 526) 173.

189. UNCLOS, Part V, Article 56.

190. See Chapter 1, Section 1.4.

191. See Chapter 2, Section 2.4; see also Kay Hailbronner (n 4) 519-520.

192. Customary International Law results from 'a general and consistent practice of States that they follow from a sense of legal obligation'; see https://www.law.cornell.edu/wex/customary_international_law accessed 5 February 2016; see on customary international law *Lotus Case (France v Turkey)* (Merits) [1927] PCIJ Rep Series A No 10; see also *North Sea Continental Shelf Cases (Federal Republic of Germany v Denmark; Federal Republic of Germany v Netherlands)* (Merits) [1969] ICJ Rep 3; see also *Nicaragua Case (Nicaragua v United States of America)* (Merits) [1986] ICJ Rep 14; see also *Gulf of Maine Case (Canada v United States)* (Merits) [1984] ICJ Rep 165; see also *Continental Shelf Case (Libyan Arab Jamahiriya v Malta)* (Merits) [1985] ICJ Rep 3.

Chapter Three

The Freedom to Lay Submarine Cables and Pipelines in the EEZ

3.1. INTRODUCTION

International law provides a developed legal framework to regulate submarine cables and pipelines. In fact, Mudrić argues that the international community also recognises the need for similar extensive regulation in relation to land-based cables and pipelines.[1] It is worth noting that submarine cables and pipelines in the territorial sea fall under the sovereignty of the coastal State and are thus regulated by the legal regime applicable to land pipelines and cables i.e. by their national legal regimes.[2] However, in other maritime zones such as the high seas and the EEZ, it is international law which governs the 'rights of laying and operation of submarine cables and pipelines, and the rights of States to oppose such undertakings'.[3]

3.2. HISTORICAL OVERVIEW: PIPELINES AND CABLES

Before examining the legal regime regulating submarine cables and pipelines it may prove useful to appreciate the origins and development of submarine cables and pipelines. The first telegraphic cables were laid down in harbours and rivers back in the 19th century.[4] Since the 1950s, telephonic cables have also been used to facilitate telephone communications.[5] Cross-country crude oil pipelines also commenced operations in the early 1900s.[6] Today copper cables have been replaced by fibre optic cables, which are generally used for internet connections.[7] According to the International Cable Protection Committee submarine telecommunication cables:

> hold the predominant role of over 95% of international voice and data traffic…Almost 100% of the transoceanic internet traffic is relayed through submarine cables.[8]

Furthermore, the author agrees with Mudrić that the demand for pipelines is expected to grow because ‘traditional source fields are being depleted’[9] and ‘new sources are often landlocked or require great transit distance’.[10]

3.3. SUBMARINE CABLES AND PIPELINES

A submarine pipeline may be defined as a ‘connected series of pipes with pumping and control devices for the carrying of liquids, gases or finely divided solids’.[11] Furthermore, cross-border pipelines may be considered as a ‘pipeline that has its origin in one nation and that traverses one or more other nations along its route’.[12]

On the other hand, underwater cables may be described as a ‘means of communication laid on the seabed between two formal points’.[13] Apart from the uses highlighted above,[14] underwater cables are also used for other purposes such as *inter alia* the detection of natural disasters[15] and for the delivery of energy. It may be argued that the term submarine cables in UNCLOS is used generically. In fact, the author notes that in all its articles on submarine cables and pipelines UNCLOS does not really distinguish between the different types of cables. In this respect it may be argued that any type of submarine cables may fall under the jurisdiction of States in terms of UNCLOS provisions. Furthermore, it may be interesting to note that the International Cable Protection Committee’s (ICPC)[16] role is to ‘provide the safeguarding of submarine telecommunications cables against manmade and natural hazards’[17] and it issued recommendations in this sense.[18] For example, ICPC Recommendation 6 of 2008 recommends actions for effective cable protection.[19] It is arguably a detailed recommendation containing specific parts on the dissemination of cable route information, stakeholder liaison and education, monitoring security of cable routes and corridors together with a legal section. For instance, the legal part of the recommendation provides for compensation for lost gear and recovery of damages. It also deals with the development of national legislation on cable protection and the establishment of ‘Cable Protection Areas’.[20]

3.4. INTERNATIONAL LEGAL FRAMEWORK FOR SUBMARINE CABLES AND PIPELINES

There are several international treaties and agreements that regulate submarine cables and pipelines. Arguably the most comprehensive in this regard is

UNCLOS. The 1958 HSC and the Geneva Convention on the Continental Shelf[21] are also relevant in relation to the laying, maintenance and protection of pipelines and cables. Other international instruments include the Convention for the Protection of Submarine Telegraph Cables[22] which is still in force for some States, 1972 Collision Regulations[23] and the 1996 Protocol to the 1972 London Convention.[24]

3.4.1. Regulations Prior to UNCLOS

What follows is an analysis of the legal regime for pipelines and cables in areas beyond national jurisdiction, pre the adoption of UNCLOS. It may be argued that prior to the adoption of the latter Convention, only a handful of international instruments regulated the laying and operation of submarine pipelines and cables beyond territorial waters.[25] It is interesting to note that these same international instruments are today still *in vigore* for certain States although it may be convincingly argued that these conventions do not correspond to the modern needs mainly because of the developments that occurred in communications since their date of adoption.[26]

3.4.1.1. Convention for the Protection of Submarine Telegraph Cables

The Convention for the Protection of Submarine Telegraph Cables establishes the freedom to lay, maintain and repair submarine cables outside of the territorial sea.[27] To safeguard the high seas freedom to lay submarine cables Article 2 of this Convention provides that:

> It is a punishable offence to break or injure a submarine cable, wilfully or by culpable negligence, in such manner as might interrupt or obstruct telegraphic communication, either wholly or partially, such punishment being without prejudice to any civil action for damages. This provision does not apply to cases where those who break or injure a cable do so with the lawful object of saving their lives or their ship, after they have taken every necessary precaution to avoid so breaking or injuring the cable.[28]

Arguably Articles 4,[29] 5,[30] 7,[31] 8,[32] 10[33] and 15[34] are the most salient provisions of this Convention being the operative parts. Article 4 of the Convention for the Protection of Submarine Telegraph Cables provided that cable owners who when laying or repairing their cable damage another existing cable must bear the repairing costs. More or less its Article 5 specified that all ships were required to stay one nautical mile (1.9 km) away from operating vessels that were laying cables. Moreover, if an owner sacrificed his/her fishing equipment in order to avoid harming a cable, he/she was entitled for compensation under Article 7 of the said Convention. Article 8 of the Convention for the Protection of Submarine Telegraph Cables specified the competent tribunals for its purposes whilst Article 10 dealt, amongst others, with the means of proof required and documentary evidence. Furthermore, Article 15 enshrined the unrestricted freedom of action of belligerents. *Prima facie* it may be argued that all the operative provisions of the Convention for the Protection of Submarine Telegraph Cables, especially key principles like the criminal responsibility of cable owners who wilfully or by culpable negligence break or injure a submarine cable, are more or less reflected in later treaties including UNCLOS in its Articles 112 to 115.

The author devoted some space to the Convention for the Protection of Submarine Telegraph Cables since the State parties to this Convention that are not parties to any of the subsequent international legislation regulating the high seas freedom of submarine cables and pipelines, like for example El Salvador, may still be bound by the provisions of this Convention. It may be argued that such States are in a detrimental position as the Convention for the Protection of Submarine Telegraph Cables was adopted in 1884 and only applies to telegraphic and power cables.

3.4.1.2. The 1958 HSC and the Continental Shelf Convention

Both the 1958 HSC and the Continental Shelf Convention 'took over relevant provisions'[35] of the Convention for the Protection of Submarine Telegraph Cables. Both Geneva Conventions cover telephone cables, high-voltage power cables and submarine pipelines.[36] Article 26 of the 1958 HSC[37] and Article 4 of the Convention of the Continental Shelf[38] are arguably the most relevant provisions in this context of submarine pipelines and cables. Both articles more or less reflect the key concepts found in the Convention for the Protection of Submarine Telegraph Cables. However, unlike the situation under the Convention for the Protection of Submarine Telegraph Cables,[39] both Geneva Conventions extended their application to submarine cables and pipelines. It may be reasonable to state that, in relation to submarine cables and pipelines, the fundamental principles contained in both Geneva Conventions are today more or less enshrined in UNCLOS.

3.4.2. UNCLOS

UNCLOS developed the articles contained in the Geneva Conventions and 'extended them significantly'.[40] UNCLOS provides express rules for the laying and operation of submarine cables and pipelines i.e. UNCLOS Articles 112 to 115.[41]

Before providing a more in-depth examination of the applicable UNCLOS provisions in relation to pipelines and cables,[42] it is worth noting what the Preamble of UNCLOS states with regards to submarine cables and pipelines. In fact, the Preamble recognises:

> the desirability of establishing through this Convention, with due regard to the sovereignty of all States, a legal order for the seas and oceans which will facilitate international communication.[43]

The United Nations' official position in this respect is also noteworthy:

> Beyond the outer limits of the 12NM territorial sea, the coastal State may not (and should not) impeded the laying or maintenance of cables, even though the delineation of the course for laying of pipelines (not cables) on the continental shelf is subject to its consent.[44]

3.5. THE FREEDOM TO LAY SUBMARINE CABLES AND PIPELINES ON THE HIGH SEAS

Article 87 of UNCLOS provides that 'all States have a right'[45] to lay submarine cables and pipelines on the bed of the high seas. Notwithstanding this right, as previously examined, the high seas remain 'open to all States'[46] and States cannot validly acquire sovereignty over 'any part of the high seas'.[47] The freedom to lay submarine cables and pipelines on the high seas gives the laying State no title whatsoever on the seabed beneath as was the case with the high seas freedoms of navigation and overflight. The high seas freedom to lay submarine cables and pipelines is also subject to the 'conditions laid down by this Convention and by other rules of international law'.[48] UNCLOS Article 87(1) expressly subjects the high seas freedom to lay submarine cables and pipelines to Part VI.[49] It results that the high seas freedom to lay submarine cables and pipelines is thus not absolute and is subject to Part VI of UNCLOS. In the author's opinion, Article 79 of UNCLOS may be considered as the central provision of Part VI,[50] to which the high seas freedom to lay submarine cables and pipelines is expressly subjected to. In the author's opinion Article 79[51] merits a detailed examination it being an expressly applicable provision to the high seas freedom to lay submarine cables and pipelines. It may thus be argued that Article 79[52] is in itself a major limitation to the same high seas freedom of pipelines and cables:

> 1. All States are entitled to lay submarine cables and pipelines on the continental shelf, in accordance with the provisions of this article.
>
> 2. Subject to its right to take reasonable measures for the exploration of the continental shelf, the exploitation of its natural resources and the prevention, reduction and control of pollution from pipelines, the coastal State may not impede the laying or maintenance of such cables or pipelines.
>
> 3. The delineation of the course for the laying of such pipelines on the continental shelf is subject to the consent of the coastal State.
>
> 4. Nothing in this Part affects the right of the coastal State to establish conditions for cables or pipelines entering its territory or territorial sea, or its jurisdiction over cables and pipelines constructed or used in connection with

> the exploration of its continental shelf or exploitation of its resources or the operations of artificial islands, installations and structures under its jurisdiction.
>
> 5. When laying submarine cables or pipelines, States shall have due regard to cables or pipelines already in position. In particular, possibilities of repairing existing cables or pipelines shall not be prejudiced.[53]

In its sub-section first Article 79[54] reiterates the right of every State to lay submarine cables and pipelines, this time on the continental shelf. It may be argued that this right includes maintenance as a freedom because this freedom must be 'exercised in accordance with the provisions of this article'[55] and UNCLOS Article 79(2) and 79(5) are specifically devoted to maintenance. Other related issues are whether the laying State has a duty to maintain the cables and pipelines and/or freely access the pipelines or cables.[56] However, the right to lay submarine cables and pipelines is constrained by the subsequent paragraphs of article 79.[57] UNCLOS Article 79(2) stipulates that coastal States 'may not impede the laying or maintenance'[58] of submarine cables and pipelines. However, the same Article 79(2)[59] permits the coastal State to 'take reasonable measures for the exploration of the continental shelf, the exploitation of its natural resources and the prevention, reduction and control of pollution from pipelines'.[60] Thus Article 79(2) of UNCLOS grants the coastal State the right to regulate pipelines within its terms. It is worth noting that in terms of Article 79(2)[61] the coastal State is granted regulation rights for the 'prevention, reduction and control of pollution'[62] from pipelines only. Article 79(2)[63] makes no reference to submarine cables. Concisely the coastal State's jurisdiction under UNCLOS Article 79(2) is very extensive. However, UNCLOS Article 79(2) subjects the coastal State's jurisdiction to 'reasonable measures'.[64] The criteria of 'reasonableness',[65] the author opines, may protect the high seas freedom to lay cables and pipelines as coastal States may not ban the laying of such submarine cables and pipelines. The coastal State's right to legislate for 'the prevention, control and reduction of pollution'[66] may for example bring about a severe restriction of the high seas freedom to 'lay submarine cables and pipelines'.[67] However, the 'reasonable measures'[68] of Article 79(2) of UNCLOS may also be considered as a caveat to protect the same high seas freedom to lay pipelines and cables from excessive intervention by the coastal State.

Furthermore, Article 79(3)[69] contains a further limitation on the high seas freedom to lay submarine pipelines. This sub-section subjects the 'delineation of the course of pipelines'[70] (not of cables) 'to the consent of the coastal State'.[71] It may be argued that this provision allows for a very serious limitation on the high seas freedom to lay pipelines. Can the coastal State thus restrict the freedom to lay pipelines by not allowing surveys of the seabed for the purpose of routing pipelines? It may be argued that if the coastal State is empowered by UNCLOS Article 79(3) to refuse pipeline surveying then the coastal State would be denying the laying State its freedom to lay submarine pipelines. Surveying the seabed for pipeline routing purposes may be considered as a complex issue. Some academics such as Lott[72] have categorised this activity as marine scientific research.[73] However, surveying may be put amongst the 'other internationally lawful uses of the sea related to...submarine cables and pipelines'[74] of Article 58(1) of UNCLOS or it may even be considered as hydrographic surveying.[75] Summarily Vinogradov argues that without a prior examination of the seabed 'the freedom to lay submarine pipelines cannot be realised in principle'.[76] In the author's opinion, the power of the coastal State to restrict pipeline surveying may thus greatly interfere with the laying State's freedom to lay pipelines.

Article 79(4)[77] takes into consideration the sovereignty of the coastal State. It preserves the coastal State's sovereignty by not regulating 'the right of the coastal State to establish conditions for...cables or pipelines entering its territory or territorial sea'.[78] Neither does Article 79(4) of UNCLOS affect the jurisdiction of the coastal State over cables and pipelines:

> constructed or used in connection with the exploration of its continental shelf or exploitation of its resources or the operation of artificial islands, installations and structures under its jurisdiction.[79]

Thus Article 79(4)[80] outlines the sovereignty of the coastal State and this in line with Articles 56,[81] 77[82] and 80.[83] The final bit of UNCLOS Article 79 i.e. Article 79(5)[84] transposes the 'due regard'[85] requirement to pipelines and cables and provides that when laying submarine cables and pipelines, other States 'shall have due regard'[86] to pipelines and cables 'already in position'.[87] This is a further protection afforded by UNCLOS to the high seas freedom to lay submarine cables and pipelines. States that previously exercised their freedom to lay submarine cables and pipelines have their right protected *vide* Article 79(5) of UNCLOS and its requirement of 'due regard'.[88] By virtue of Article 79(5) of UNCLOS laying States are required to protect the submarine cables and pipelines that other States previously laid by exercising their freedom. Furthermore, there is a specific reference to maintenance and as such 'possibilities of repairing existing cables or pipelines shall not be prejudiced'.[89] Therefore, the owner of the cable or pipeline to be laid has to pay 'due regard'[90] to other pipelines and cables already in position. As Mudrić argues UNCLOS makes it a duty to inform 'an owner of the already existing submarine cable or pipeline in the case of crossing'[91] and even an 'obligation of negotiation regarding the point of crossing if necessary'.[92]

Since Article 87[93] expressly subjects the highs seas freedom to lay pipelines and cables to Part VI,[94] a quick reference to the remaining provisions of the same Part VI[95] will follow. Article 76[96] gives a comprehensive definition of the continental shelf which is of little relevance to submarine cables and pipelines.[97] The same is arguably the case with Article 77[98] which specifies the coastal State's rights over the continental shelf. Article 78[99] especially its section 78(1) more or less reflects the position in the EEZ. However, little is there to say about Articles 80 to 85[100] and their relevance to the high seas freedom to lay pipelines and cables in the EEZ. Notwithstanding this, it may be observed that UNCLOS contains certain specific articles on 'artificial islands, installations and structures'[101] including Article 80[102] as distinct from other specific provisions on submarine cables and pipelines. This structure suggests that submarine cables and pipelines do not fall within the 'artificial islands, installations and structures'[103] category. It is noteworthy that the provisions of other international instruments such as the 2001 UNESCO Underwater Cultural Heritage Convention[104] may be understood to suggest otherwise. In fact, Article 1(1)(b)[105] of the 2001 UNESCO Convention provides that submarine cables are not underwater cultural heritage within the scope of the Convention and it refers to 'installations other than pipelines and cables',[106] thus suggesting that cables and pipelines are part of the wider class of installations.

Furthermore, it may be argued that Article 87(2)[107] further limits the high seas freedom to lay submarine cables and pipelines. By virtue of Article 87(2) of UNCLOS the 'due regard'[108] requirement is also applicable to the freedom to lay submarine cables and pipelines on the high seas. This was also the case with the freedoms of navigation and overflight on the high seas.[109] *In breve* this freedom shall be exercised with 'due regard'[110] for the interests of other States in their exercise of the freedom of the high seas and also with 'due regard'[111] for the rights under UNCLOS 'with respect to activities in the Area'.[112]

UNCLOS Articles 112 to 115 also deal specifically and expressly with the high seas freedom to lay submarine cables and pipelines. Article 112 of UNCLOS makes it clear that all States are entitled to lay submarine cables and pipelines on the bed of the high seas beyond the continental shelf.[113] As Takei argues cables and pipelines on the bed of the high seas but within the continental shelf are thus outside the scope of Article 112.[114] However, it is worth noting that Article 58(2) of UNCLOS makes this position applicable to the EEZ. It is also noteworthy that the Virginia Commentary suggests that 'all States'[115] is not to be read restrictively and the term refers to the right of States or 'their nationals to lay cables'.[116]

Articles 113 to 115 of UNCLOS deal with the protection of submarine cables and pipelines. In particular Articles 113 and 114 of UNCLOS regulate cables beneath the high seas.[117] Therefore, Articles 113 and 114 of UNCLOS may apply to submarine cables and pipelines on the continental shelf and pipelines and cables in the Area. UNCLOS Article 113 makes it clear that every State shall adopt the laws and regulations necessary with regards to criminal responsibility for cable breaking.[118] In other words every State is required by Article 113 of UNCLOS to have national legislation regarding the punishment of the breaking or injury of a submarine cable or pipeline by a ship flying its flag or by a person subject to its jurisdiction.[119] As Takei's argues this provision applies to 'conduct calculated or likely to result in such breaking or injury'.[120] It is interesting to compare this provision with Article 27 of the High Seas Convention which *prima facie* is very similar:

> Every State shall take the necessary legislative measures to provide that the breaking or injury by a ship flying its flag or by a person subject to its jurisdiction of a submarine cable beneath the high seas done wilfully or through culpable negligence, in such a manner as to be liable to interrupt or obstruct telegraphic or telephonic communications, and similarly the breaking or injury of a submarine pipeline or high-voltage power cable shall be a punishable offence. This provision shall not apply to any break or injury caused by persons who acted merely with the legitimate object of saving their lives or their ships, after having taken all necessary precautions to avoid such break or injury.[121]

However, it is noteworthy that UNCLOS has developed Article 27 of the 1958 HSC and included an additional requirement i.e. '[t]his provision shall apply also to conduct calculated or likely to result in such breaking or injury'.[122] Before this UNCLOS addition cable owners were precluded from taking legal action until actual cable damage occurred. The addition introduced further protection to submarine cables and pipelines by allowing preventive legal action. Beckman states that Article 113 of UNCLOS is not widely implemented by States and hence, according to him, it may not reflect customary international law.[123] In the author's opinion, irrespective whether this provision is widely implemented by each State or not, Article 113[124] grants States wide room for discretion and this alone may impact the high seas freedom to lay submarine cables and pipelines. This may be especially the case when considering that in terms of UNCLOS Article 113 States are empowered to determine how to punish the offenders.

UNCLOS Article 114 relates to the cost bearing of pipeline and cable owners if during the laying or repairing of their pipeline or cable an existing cable or pipeline is injured or broken.[125] Article 115 of UNCLOS concerns the indemnification for nets, anchors and other fishing equipment which in order to avoid injuring a submarine cable or pipeline is sacrificed.[126] The laws and regulations adopted by the coastal State in terms of Articles 114 and 115 of UNCLOS are aimed at protecting the high seas freedom to lay submarine cables and pipelines. However, if done to an excessive extent the high seas freedom to lay submarine cables and pipelines may be impacted negatively.[127]

3.6. THE FREEDOM TO LAY SUBMARINE CABLES AND PIPELINES IN THE EEZ

The EEZ concept includes both superjacent waters and seabed and its subsoil and thus there is an 'overlap between the EEZ and the continental shelf up to the outer limit of the 200-mile zone'.[128] The author is for this reason to draw parallelism between the EEZ and the continental shelf. UNCLOS recognises the freedom to lay 'submarine cables and pipelines'[129] both in the EEZ *vide* Article 58[130] and the continental shelf *vide* Article 79.[131] In the EEZ all States enjoy the freedom of, *inter alia*, 'the laying of submarine cables or pipelines and other internationally lawful uses of the sea related to these freedoms',[132] such as those associated with the operation of submarine pipelines or cables.[133] It may be argued that this EEZ freedom is not absolute and is further limited than the high seas freedom to lay submarine cables and pipelines as it exists within the limits of the coastal State's sovereign rights of Article 56.[134] The EEZ's freedom to lay submarine cables and pipelines is also subject to UNCLOS Article 58(2), and thus is expressly subject to UNCLOS Articles 88 to 115 and 'other pertinent rules of international law'[135] also apply to the EEZ 'in so far as they are not incompatible with this Part'.[136] Therefore, it is noteworthy that by virtue of UNCLOS Article 58(2) provisions 112 to 115[137] of the high seas in particular apply *mutatis mutandis* to the freedom to lay submarine cables and pipelines in the EEZ.[138] Furthermore, in terms of UNCLOS Article 58(3) in exercising their rights States shall have 'due regard'[139] to the rights and duties of the coastal State as was the case with the freedoms of navigation and overflight in the EEZ.[140]

It may be argued that the limitations of Article 79[141] are also very relevant in an EEZ context and this due to the overlap between the EEZ and continental shelf.[142] In particular coastal States may impede the laying or maintenance of cables to the extent of its right to take reasonable measures for the exploration of the continental shelf and the exploitation of its natural resources.[143] Such measures may also be taken for the prevention, reduction and control of pollution from pipelines (not cables).[144] In an EEZ context Article 79(3)[145] in particular merits an added emphasis due to its possible negative effects on the freedom to lay submarine cables in the EEZ. Coastal States may not impose UNCLOS Article 79(3) and its requirement of 'coastal State consent'[146] on the laying of submarine cables.[147] However, this does not imply that the coastal State's consent is not required at all times. For example, routes for submarine cables on the continental shelf may be subject to the coastal State's consent if they pass through the territorial sea.[148] Concisely UNCLOS Article 79(3) may not only limit the high seas freedom to lay submarine pipelines in the EEZ in cases of no forthcoming coastal State's 'consent to the delineation'[149] but also the realm of submarine cables in the EEZ may be affected and limited. In fact, some coastal States like Malaysia,[150] India,[151] China[152] and Pakistan[153] adopted liberal undertakings to the extent that the coastal State's 'consent to the delineation'[154] is applied to both submarine cables and pipelines. Authors like Acker and Hodgson argue that this approach is perfectly justified.[155] It may be argued that such an approach burdens the high seas freedom to lay cables in the EEZ as the express pipeline limits of UNCLOS Article 79(3) are applied to it simply by analogy.

For completion's sake Part XV of UNCLOS caters for the dispute settlement process. The compulsory dispute resolution mechanism also covers disputes with regards to the freedom to lay submarine cables and pipelines as specified in Article 58.[156] Summarily Article 297[157] accords submarine cables and pipelines the highest level of dispute resolution protection.

3.7. CONCLUSION

States enjoy the freedom to lay submarine cables and pipelines in the EEZ together with 'other internationally lawful uses of the sea related to'[158] this freedom compatible with the other provisions of UNCLOS,[159] such as the freedoms of navigation and overflight in the EEZ, which is subject to two important restrictions mainly the 'due regard'[160] for the interests of other States and Articles 88 to 115 of UNCLOS, with UNCLOS Articles 112 to 115 being especially important limitations in this particular context. A further express limitation is found in Article 79,[161] which is applicable to the EEZ because the seabed of the EEZ is coterminous with the continental shelf. In particular, UNCLOS Article 79(3) may severely impact the freedom to lay pipelines (and arguably cables) in the EEZ. Churchill and Lowe question the compatibility of UNCLOS Article 79(3) with the freedom to lay pipelines and argue that the use of the term 'freedom'[162] is in this context perhaps 'misleading'.[163] In view of the above limitations, it may be reasonable to conclude that the right of other States to lay cables and pipelines in the EEZ of another coastal State is more restricted than their corresponding right to lay pipelines and cables on the high seas. This is even more so with UNCLOS Article 58(3) which requires other States to exercise their right to lay pipelines and cables in a coastal State's EEZ with 'due regard'[164] and comply with:

> the laws and regulations adopted by the coastal State in accordance with the provisions of this Convention and other rules of international law in so far as they are not incompatible with this Part.[165]

NOTES

1. Mišo Mudrić, "Rights of States Regarding Underwater Cables and Pipelines" *Australian Resources and Energy Law Journal* (2010) 235.

2. Ibid.

3. Ibid; see also UNCLOS, Part VII, Articles 112 to 115; see in general Thomas Menash, "Submarine Cables and the International Law of the Sea" in Lilian del Castillo, *Law of the Sea, From Grotius to the International Tribunal for the Law of the Sea* (Brill Nijhoff, 2015) 725-731.

4. Ibid.

5. Yoshinobu Takei, 'Law and Policy for International Submarine Cables in the Asia-Pacific Region' (2011) Asian Society of International Law Working Paper 2010/13, 1-24 http://www.asiansil.org/index.php?option=com_publications&Itemid=62 accessed 18 March 2016.

6. Mišo Mudrić (n 1) 235-236.

7. Ibid.

8. Ibid.

9. Ibid.

10. Ibid.

11. Rainer Lagoni, "Pipelines" in Rudolf Berhnardt, *Max Planck Encyclopedia of Public International Law* (Oxford University Press, 1992) 1033-1034; see also *Hepburn Act* of 1906, an early United States law on the subject, which defined pipelines as 'common carriers'; see in general Cooper John Milton, *Pivotal Decades: The United States: 1900-1920* (New York: Norton, 1990); see in general Eisner Mark Allen, *Regulatory Politics in Transition* (Johns Hopkins University Press, 2000); see in general Kolko Gabriel, *Railroads and Regulation 1877-1916* (Princeton University Press, 1965). It is also worth noting that although submarine pipelines in the territory of a State are subject to that State's sovereignty there are various international rules that apply to land-based pipelines. Examples of such international rules include: (a) General Agreement on Tariffs and Trade (GATT); see General Agreement on Tariffs and Trade (adopted 30 October 1947, entered into force 1 January 1948) 55 UNTS 194; see also the GATT documentation at the CIESIN Thematic Guide www.ciesin.org accessed 18 March 2016; (b) 1921 Barcelona Convention and 1921 Barcelona Statute on the Freedom of Transit; see Barcelona Convention and Statue on Freedom of Transit (adopted 20 April 1921, entered 31 October 1922) and the (c) Convention on Transit Trade of Land-Locked States 1965; see Convention on Transit Trade of Land-Locked States (adopted 8 July 1965, entered 9 June 1967) 597 UNTS 3.

12. Michael Dulaney and Robert Merrick, "Legal Issues in Cross-Border Oil and Gas Pipelines" *Journal of Energy and Natural Resources Law* (2005) 247.

13. Rainer Lagoni, "Cables, Submarine" in Rudolf Berhnardt, *Max Planck Encyclopedia of Public International Law* (Oxford University Press, 1992) 516-519.

14. See Chapter 3, Section 3.2.

15. Rainer Lagoni (n 11) 1033-1034.

16. The International Cable Protection Committee (ICPC) is an international organisation made up of profit-making cable companies and governmental administrations.

17. See www.iscpc.org accessed 18 March 2016.

18. It may be argued that some of the most relevant recommendations in this context are: (a) Cable Routing and Reporting Criteria; see ICPC Recommendation 2 (2008) https://www.iscpc.org/publications/recommendations/ accessed 18 March 2016; (b) Telecommunications Cable and Oil Pipeline / Power Cables Crossing Criteria; see ICPC Recommendation 3 (2008) https://www.iscpc.org/publications/recommendations/ accessed 18 March 2016; and (c) Actions for Effective Cable Protection (Post Installation); see ICPC Recommendation 6 (2008) https://www.iscpc.org/publications/recommendations/ accessed 18 March 2016.

19. Ibid, Recommendation 6 (2008).

20. Ibid.

21. Convention on the Continental Shelf (adopted 29 April 1958, entered into force 10 June 1964) 499 UNTS 311, hereinafter referred to as the Continental Shelf Convention; see in general on the continental shelf Sir Cecil Hurst, "Whose is the Bed of the Sea?" *British Yearbook of International Law* 4 (1923-1924) 34-43; see also J. A. C. Gutteridge, "The 1958 Convention on the Continental Shelf" *British Yearbook of International Law* 35 (1959) 102-123; see also Martinus Willem Mouton, *The Continental Shelf* (Martinus Nijhoff Publishers, 1952); see also Zdenek J. Slouka, *International Custom and the Continental Shelf: A Study in*

the Dynamics of Customary Rules of International Law (Martinus Nijhoff Publishers, 2012); see also Marjorie M. Whiteman, "Conference on the Law of the Sea: Convention on the Continental Shelf" *American Journal of International Law* 52 (1958) 629-660; see also Ted L. McDorman, "The Continental Shelf" in Donald Rothwell, Alex Oude Elferink, Karen Scott and Tim Stephens, *The Oxford Handbook of the Law of the Sea* (Oxford University Press, 2015) 181-202.

22. Convention for the Protection of Submarine Telegraph Cables (adopted 14 March 1884, entered into force 1 May 1888) TS 380.

23. Convention on the International Regulations for Prevention Collisions at Sea (adopted 20 October 1972, entered into force 15 July 1977) 1050 UNTS 16.

24. 1996 Protocol to the Convention on the Prevention of Marine Pollution by Dumping of Wastes and Other Matter of 29 December 1972 (adopted 7 November 1996, entered into force 24 March 2006) 2006 ATS 11.

25. Mainly the Convention for the Protection of Submarine Telegraph Cables, the 1958 HSC and the Continental Shelf Convention; see Chapter 3, Sections 3.4.1.1. and 3.4.1.2.

26. See Chapter 3, Sections 3.4.1.1. and 3.4.1.2.

27. Convention on the Protection of Submarine Telegraph Cables, Article 1.

28. Ibid, Article 2.

29. The owner of a cable who, on laying or repairing his own cable, breaks or injures another cable, must bear the cost of repairing the breakage or injury, without prejudice to the application, if need by, of Article II of the present Convention; see ibid Article 4.

30. Vessels engaged in laying or repairing submarine cables shall conform to the regulations as to signals which have been, or may be, adopted by mutual agreement among the High Contracting Parties, with the view of preventing collisions at sea.

When a ship engaged in repairing a cable exhibits the said signals, other vessels which see them, or are able to see them, shall withdraw to or keep beyond a distance of one nautical mile at least from the ship in question, so as not to interfere with her operations.

Fishing gear and nets shall be kept at the same distance.

Nevertheless, fishing vessels which see, or are able to see, a telegraph-ship exhibiting the said signals, shall be allowed a period of 24 hours at most within which to obey the notice so given, during which time they shall not be interfered with in any way.

The operations of the telegraph-ships shall be completed as quickly as possible; see ibid Article 5.

31. Owners of ships or vessels who can prove that they have sacrificed an anchor, a net, or other fishing gear in order to avoid injuring a submarine cable, shall receive compensation from the owner of the cable.

In order to establish a claim to such compensation, a statement, supported by the evidence of the crew, should, whenever possible, be drawn up immediately after the occurrence; and the master must, within 24 hours after his return to or next putting into port, make a declaration to the proper authorities.

The latter shall communicate the information to the consular authorities of the country to which the owner of the cable belongs; see ibid Article 7.

32. The tribunals competent to take cognizance of infractions of the present Convention are those of the country to which the vessel on board of which the offence was committed belongs.

It is, moreover, understood that, in cases where the provisions in the previous paragraph cannot apply, offences against the present Convention will be dealt with in each of the Contracting States in accordance, so far as the subjects and citizens of those States respectively are concerned, with the general rules of criminal jurisdiction prescribed by the laws of that particular State, or by international treaties; see ibid Article 8.

33. Offences against the present Convention may be verified by all means of proof allowed by the legislation of the country of the court. When the officers commanding the ships of war, or ships specially commissioned for the purpose by one of the High Contracting Parties, have reason to believe that an infraction of the measures provided for in the present Convention has been committed by a vessel other than a vessel of war, they may demand from the captain or master the production of the official documents proving the nationality of the said vessel. The fact of such document having been exhibited shall then be endorsed upon it immediately.

Further, formal statements of the facts may be prepared by the said officers, whatever may be the nationality of the vessel incriminated. These formal statements shall be drawn up in the form and in the language used in the country to which the officer making them belongs; they may be considered, in the country where they are adduced, as evidence in accordance with the laws of that country. The accused and the witnesses shall have the right to add, or to have added thereto, in their own language, any explanations they may consider useful. These declarations shall be duly signed; see ibid Article 10.

34. It is understood that the stipulations of the present Convention do not in any way restrict the freedom of action of belligerents; see ibid Article 15.

35. See Robert Beckman, "Submarine Cables – A Critically Important but Neglected Area of the Law of the Sea" (7TH International Conference on Legal Regimes of Sea, Air, Space and Antarctica, New Delhi, January 2010).

36. See Réne Jean Dupuy and Daniel Vignes, *A Handbook on the New Law of the Sea: Volume II* (Martinus Nijhoff Publishers, 1991) 977-988.

37. 1. All States shall be entitled to lay submarine cables and pipelines on the bed of the high seas.

2. Subject to its right to take reasonable measures for the exploration of the continental shelf and the exploitation of its natural resources, the coastal State may not impede the laying or maintenance of such cables or pipelines.

3. When laying such cables or pipelines the State in question shall pay due regard to cables or pipelines already in position on the seabed. In particular, possibilities of repairing existing cables or pipelines shall not be prejudiced; see 1958 HSC, Article 26.

38. Subject to its right to take reasonable measures for the exploration of the continental shelf and the exploitation of its natural resources, the coastal State may not impede the laying or maintenance of submarine cables or pipe lines on the continental shelf; see Continental Shelf Convention, Article 4.

39. It only covered submarine telegraph cables.

40. Mišo Mudrić (n 1) 248-252.

41. See Rainer Lagoni, *Legal Aspects of High Voltage Direct Current (HVDC) Cables* (LIT Verlag, 1999); see also John Crowley, "International Law and Coastal State Control over the Laying of Submarine Pipelines on the Continental Shelf" *Nordic Journal of International Law* (1987) 40.

42. See Chapter 3, Section 3.5.

43. UNCLOS, Preamble.

44. Answer to FAQ 7 at United Nations website; see http://www.un.org/Depts/los/LEGISLATIONANDTREATIES/frequently_asked_questions.htm accessed 18 March 2016.

45. UNCLOS, Part VII, Section 1, Article 87.

46. Ibid.

47. Ibid, Article 89.

48. Ibid, Article 87; see Chapter 1, Section 1.3.

49. UNCLOS, Part VI, Article 76 to 85.

50. Ibid.

51. Ibid, Article 79.

52. Ibid.

53. Ibid; The burying of pipelines and cables in the subsoil of the seabed (one mode of installing cables and pipelines) is a moot point in UNCLOS. It may be argued that for UNCLOS purposes 'laying' (see UNCLOS, Part VI, Article 79) and burying are equivalent. However, the coastal State has exclusive control and authority if the burying of pipelines and cables is categorised as 'drilling' (see UNCLOS, Part VI, Article 81). Furthermore, it is noteworthy that under article 58(1) of UNCLOS all States enjoy 'other internationally lawful uses of the sea related to these freedoms, such as those associated with…submarine cables and pipelines' (see UNCLOS, Part V, Article 58(1)) in the EEZ.

54. UNCLOS, Part VI, Article 79.

55. Ibid, Article 79(1).

56. See Robert Beckman (n 35) 5-6; see also Martha M. Roggenkamp, "Petroleum Pipelines in the North Sea: Questions of Jurisdiction and Practical Solutions" *Journal of Energy and*

Natural Resources Law (1998) 97-98; see also Patricia Birnie, Alan Boyle and Catherine Redgwell, *International Law and the Environment* (Oxford University Press, 2009) 147; see also John Crowley (n 41) 52.

57. UNCLOS, Part VI, Article 79.
58. Ibid, Article 79(2).
59. Ibid.
60. Ibid.
61. Ibid.
62. Ibid.
63. Ibid.
64. Ibid.
65. See Sergei Vinogradov, "Challenges of Nord Stream: Streamlining International Legal Frameworks and Regimes for Submarine Pipelines" *German Yearbook of International Law* (2009) 282; see also Robert Beckman (n 35) 6; see also Alexander Lott, "Marine Environmental Protection and Transboundary Pipeline Projects: A Case Study of the Nord Stream Pipeline" *Utrecht Journal of International and European Law* (2011) 58; see also Tara Davenport "Submarine Communications Cables and Law of the Sea: Problems in Law and Practice" *Ocean Development and International Law* (2012) 211.
66. UNCLOS, Part VI, Article 79(2).
67. Ibid, Part VII, Section 1, Article 87(1); see also Alan Boyle, "Further Development of the 1982 Convention on the Law of the Sea: Mechanisms for Change" *International and Comparative Law Quarterly* (2005) 569; see also Donald Rothwell and Tim Stephens, *The International Law of the Sea* (Hart Publishing Ltd, 2010) 359-362; see also Alexander Proelss, "Pipelines and Protected Sea Areas" in Richard Caddell and Thomas Rhidian, *Shipping, Law and the Marine Environment in the 21st Century: Emerging Challenges for the Law of the Sea – Legal Implications and Liabilities* (Lawtext Publishing Ltd, 2013) 276; see also Skirmante Klumbyte, "Environment Protection: Pipelines" in Ulrich Karpen *Maritime Safety – Current Problems of Use of the Baltic Sea: Conference in Cooperation with the International Tribunal for the Law of the Sea April 21st – 23rd, 2004* (Nomos Publishing House, 2004) 75.
68. UNCLOS, Part VI, Article 79(2).
69. Ibid.
70. Ibid.
71. Ibid.
72. Alexander Lott (n 65) 59-61.
73. See Annick De Marffy, "Marine Scientific Research" in Réne Jean Dupuy and Daniel Vignes, *A Handbook on the New Law of the Sea: Volume 2* (Martinus Nijhoff Publishers, 1991) 1128-1131; see also Patricia Birnie, "Law of the Sea and Ocean Resources: Implications for Marine Scientific Research" *International Journal of Marine and Coastal Law* (1995) 242.
74. UNCLOS, Part V, Article 58(1).
75. Sam Bateman, "Hydrographic Surveying in the EEZ: Differences and Overlaps with Marine Scientific Research" *Marine Policy* (2005) 170-172.
76. Sergei Vinogradov (n 65) 282.
77. UNCLOS, Part VI, Article 79(4).
78. Ibid.
79. Ibid.
80. Ibid.
81. UNCLOS Article 56 deals with the rights, jurisdiction and duties of the coastal State in the EEZ.
82. 1. The coastal State exercises over the continental shelf sovereign rights for the purpose of exploring it and exploiting its natural resources.

2. The rights referred to in paragraph 1 are exclusive in the sense that if the coastal State does not explore the continental shelf or exploit its natural resources, no one may undertake these activities without the express consent of the coastal State.

3. The rights of the coastal State over the continental shelf do not depend on occupation, effective or notional, or on any express proclamation.

4. The natural resources referred to in this Part consist of the mineral and other non-living resources of the seabed and subsoil together with living organisms belonging to sedentary species, that is to say, organisms which, at the harvestable stage, either are immobile on or under the seabed or are unable to move except in constant physical contact with the seabed or the subsoil; see UNCLOS, Part VI, Article 77.

83. Article 60 applies *mutatis mutandis* to artificial islands, installations and structures on the continental shelf; see ibid, Article 80.

84. Ibid, Article 79(5).

85. Ibid, Part VII, Section 1, Article 87(2); see Chapter 1, Section 1.3.1.

86. Ibid, Part VI, Article 79(5).

87. Ibid.

88. Ibid.

89. Ibid.

90. Ibid.

91. Mišo Mudrić (n 1) 248-252.

92. Ibid.

93. UNCLOS, Part VII, Section 1, Article 87.

94. Ibid, Part VI, Article 76 to 85.

95. Ibid.

96. Ibid, Part VI, Article 76.

97. It is worth emphasising that the definition of the continental shelf contained in Article 76 of UNCLOS may be indirectly relevant to the general subject of this book because the high seas extend to the seabed and subsoil subject to the UNCLOS provisions on the outer continental shelf beyond the EEZ and also Part XI of UNCLOS. However, it is of little relevance to the freedom to lay submarine cables and pipelines.

98. Ibid, Article 77.

99. Ibid, Article 78.

100. Ibid, Articles 80 to 85.

101. Ibid, Article 80.

102. Ibid.

103. Ibid.

104. UNESCO Convention on the Protection of the Underwater Cultural Heritage (adopted 2 November 2001, entered into force 2 January 2009) 2562 UNTS 1, hereinafter referred to as the 2001 UNESCO Convention.

105. (b) Pipelines and cables placed on the seabed shall not be considered as underwater cultural heritage.

106. Ibid, Article 1(1)(c).

107. UNCLOS, Part VII, Section 1, Article 87(2).

108. Ibid.

109. See Chapter 1, Section 1.3.

110. Ibid.

111. Ibid.

112. Ibid.

113. 1. All States are entitled to lay submarine cables and pipelines on the bed of the high seas beyond the continental shelf.

2. Article 79, paragraph 5, applies to such cables and pipelines.

114. UNCLOS, Part VII, Section 1, Article 112; see Yoshinobu Takei (n 5) 2-10.

115. Ibid.

116. John Norton Moore, Myron H. Nordquist, Satya N. Nandan and Shabtai Rosenne, *United Nations Convention on the Law of the Sea 1982: A Commentary* (Martinus Nijhoff Publishers, 1993), Volume VII 264.

117. UNCLOS, Part VII, Section 1, Articles 113 and 114.

118. Ibid, Article 113.

119. Ibid.

120. Yoshinobu Takei (n 5) 2-10.

121. Ibid.

122. UNCLOS, Part VII, Section 1, Article 113.
123. See Robert Beckman (n 35) 14.
124. Ibid.
125. Ibid, Article 114.
126. Ibid, Article 115; Article 115 makes no reference to any maritime zone, however, considering its location (i.e. under Part VII), it is reasonable to assume that UNCLOS article 115 is concerned with the high seas.
127. For the sake of completion UNCLOS does not allow a general right of visit on the high seas. The right of visit is provided for in UNCLOS Article 110. Article 21 of the 1958 HSC corresponds to UNCLOS Article 110. It consists of the right to board a foreign vessel on the high seas (or EEZ) only if there is 'reasonable ground for suspecting' that the foreign vessel is engaged in slave trade or piracy. The right of visit may only be exercised by 'warships' (including military aircraft) and by 'all other ships or aircraft clearly marked and identifiable as being on government service and authorized to that effect'; see UNCLOS, Part VII, Section 1, Article 110; see also Réne Jean Dupuy and Daniel Vignes (n 36) 847-863.
128. Yoshinobu Takei (n 5) 4.
129. UNCLOS, Part V, Article 58.
130. Ibid.
131. Ibid, Part VI, Article 79.
132. Ibid, Part V, Article 58.
133. Ibid.
134. Ibid, Article 56.
135. Ibid, Article 58(2).
136. Ibid.; see Chapter 1, Section 1.4.
137. Ibid, Part VII, Section 1, Articles 112 to 115.
138. See Chapter 1, Section 1.4.
139. Ibid, Part V, Article 58(3).
140. Furthermore, it is worth noting that UNCLOS Article 300 provides for *bona fide* and abuse of rights.; see Chapter 1, Section 1.4.
141. UNCLOS, Part VI, Article 79.
142. See Chapter 3, Section 3.5.
143. Ibid; see also Robert Beckman (n 35) 9-10.
144. Ibid; it is interesting to compare UNCLOS Article 79(2) with Article 26(2) of the 1958 HSC and Article 4 of the Continental Shelf Convention.
145. UNCLOS, Part VI, Article 79(3).
146. Ibid.
147. This view is also reflected in the drafting history of this provision; see Seabed Committee 1973 Session Proposal A/AC.138/SC.II/L.34 by China; see also John Norton Moore, Myron H. Nordquist, Satya N. Nandan and Shabtai Rosenne (n 116) Volume II 911-915.
148. Yoshinobu Takei (n 5) 2-10.
149. UNCLOS, Part VI, Article 79(3).
150. Exclusive Economic Zone Act (Malaysia), Article 22(1).
151. The Territorial Waters, Continental Shelf, Exclusive Economic Zone and Other Maritime Zones Act (India), Article 6(7).
152. Exclusive Economic Zone and Continental Shelf Act (China), Article 11; see also Regulations on Management of Laying Submarine Cables and Pipelines (China), Article 4(3).
153. Territorial Waters and Maritime Zones Act (Pakistan), Articles 5(6) and 6(6).
154. UNCLOS, Part VI, Article 79(3).
155. Hendrick Acker and Stephen Hodgson, *Legal Aspects of Maritime Spatial Planning* (Fish/2006/09) 55.
156. UNCLOS, Part V, Article 58.
157. Ibid, Part XV, Section 3, Article 297.
158. Ibid, Part V, Article 58(1).
159. Ibid.
160. Ibid, Article 58.
161. Ibid, Part VI, Article 79(3).

162. Ibid.
163. Robin Churchill and Alan Vaughn Lowe, *The Law of the Sea* (Manchester University Press, 1988) 133-152.
164. UNCLOS, Part V, Article 58(3).
165. Ibid.

Conclusions

The essence of the freedom of the high seas is that no State may acquire sovereignty over parts of them.[1] Article 87 of UNCLOS provides that the high seas are open to all States and that the freedom of the high seas is exercised under the conditions laid down in UNCLOS and by other rules of international law. It includes *inter alia* the freedoms of navigation, overflight and the laying of submarine cables and pipelines. Such freedoms are to be exercised with 'due regard'[2] for the interests of other States in their exercise of the freedom of the high seas, and also with 'due regard'[3] for the rights under UNCLOS regarding activities in the International Seabed Area.[4]

The evolution of the EEZ raised important issues about its relationship with the high seas.[5] It may be argued that UNCLOS Articles 58, 86 and 87 are crucial to analyse the relationship between the EEZ and the high seas regime.[6] This book examined the relationship between the high seas regime and the EEZ by separately analysing the freedom of navigation, overflight and laying of submarine cables and pipelines.[7] The waters of the EEZ remain, as a general rule, open to all States. However, under UNCLOS Article 56, the coastal State is granted *inter alia* 'sovereign rights'[8] for the purposes therein specified i.e. 'for the purpose of exploring and exploiting, conserving and managing natural resources, whether living or non-living…'.[9] The 'sovereign rights'[10] of UNCLOS Article 56, are not applicable on the high seas, and additionally restrict the freedom of navigation, overflight and laying of submarine cables and pipelines in the EEZ. Furthermore, Article 58 of UNCLOS lays down the rights and duties of other States in the EEZ. Basically, these are the high seas freedom of navigation, overflight and laying of submarine cables and pipelines. Article 58 of UNCLOS also provides that in exercising their rights and performing their duties, States should have 'due regard'[11] to the rights, duties and laws of the coastal State.

The high seas freedoms of navigation, overflight and laying of submarine cables and pipelines characterise the relationship between the high seas regime and the EEZ. It is submitted that all three freedoms i.e. the freedom of navigation, overflight and laying of submarine cables and pipelines apply in the EEZ yet to a more limited extent mainly because of the 'sovereign rights'[12] coastal States enjoy in the EEZ.

The 'traditional and well-recognised facet of the doctrine of the high seas'[13] i.e. the freedom of navigation is applicable in the EEZ. It is subject to a number of limitations. For example, the freedom of navigation shall be exercised by States with 'due regard' for the interests of other States exercising the freedom of navigation, but also with regard to the rights under UNCLOS and to activities in the Area.[14] Furthermore, Articles 88 to 115 of UNCLOS together with other relevant rules of international law which deal with navigation on the high seas may further burden the freedom of navigation in the EEZ.[15] Moreover, it may be argued that in the EEZ there are specific limitations that restrict the freedom of navigation. For instance, foreign shipping is arguably subject to the pollution control powers of the coastal State.[16] Even artificial islands and installations may affect navigation in the EEZ.[17] It may be argued that UNCLOS provides a detailed and comprehensive regime which adequately protects the freedom of navigation in the EEZ. However, certain issues like for example naval manoeuvres and weapons practice may give rise to ambiguities which in turn may threaten the freedom of navigation in the EEZ.[18] Further harmonising national EEZ decrees may bring about more uniformity between States and hence the possibility of greater protection to the freedom of navigation in the EEZ.

Like the freedom of navigation in the EEZ, the freedom of overflight in the EEZ is arguably more restricted than the high seas freedom of overflight.[19] Not only is the freedom of overflight in the EEZ subject to the 'due regard'[20] for other States and Articles 88 to 115 of UNCLOS but it may possibly be subject to additional limitations. For example, coastal States may control aircraft *vide* their competence to regulate waste dumping.[21] Even artificial islands and installations constructed by the coastal State may for example obstacle low flying in their vicinity.[22] With regards to the freedom of overflight in the EEZ a number of uncertainties may also arise. For example, it is unclear which rules of the air apply to aircraft in the EEZ.[23] It is arguably unclear whether aircraft in the EEZ are subject to ICAO's Rules of the Air or to the territorial regulations of States.[24] Uncertainty, may also arise in relation to military overflight. To what extent can foreign military aircraft use the EEZ for military exercises? UNCLOS does not always give straightforward answers to such questions. It may be argued that this uncertainty may unfortunately affect the freedom of overflight in the EEZ negatively.[25] A balance between the jurisdictional claims of the coastal States and freedom of overflight in the EEZ has to be achieved and this in the interest of the freedom of the air itself.

All States enjoy the rights of laying submarine pipelines and cables in the EEZ. However, this is arguably to a more limited extent than on the high seas.[26] Apart from the explicit high seas limitations to which the other freedoms are subject,[27] this freedom is additionally subject to Articles 112 to 115 of UNCLOS. Moreover, an explicit limitation is further contained in Article 79 of UNCLOS.[28] Although in the EEZ the coastal State may only object to the laying and operation of cables and pipelines if they seriously prejudice the rights of exploitation and exploration of the natural resources of the zone, it may be argued that this is a wide enough power to affect the freedom to lay pipelines and cables in the EEZ negatively if applied excessively.[29] All State Parties to UNCLOS should make sure that their legislation is fully compliant with the specific pipeline and cable obligations,[30] and this to protect the freedom to lay submarine cables and pipelines in the EEZ.

NOTES

1. That is the general rule. However, it may be subject to exceptions. For example, certain areas of the high seas adjacent to the territorial waters of coastal States may become subject to that State's sovereignty. See *Anglo-Norwegian Fisheries Case (United Kingdom v Norway)* (Merits) [1951] ICJ Rep 3; see also Malcolm N. Shaw, *International Law* (Cambridge University Press, 2014) 441-452.
2. UNCLOS, Part VII, Section 1, Article 87(2).
3. Ibid.
4. See in general on the International Seabed Area Sir Robert Jennings and Sir Arthur Watts, *Oppenheim's International Law* (Oxford University Press, 2008) 812; see also Evan Luard, *The Control of the Sea-Bed: A New International Issue* (Taplinger Publishers, 1974); see also Barry Buzan, *Seabed Politics* (Greenwood Publishing Group, 1976); see also Nguyen Quoc Dinh, Patrick Daillier and Alain Pellet, *Droit International Public* (LGDJ 2002) 1210; see also Richard Young, "The Legal Regime of the Deep Sea Floor" *American Journal of International Law* 62 (1968) 641-653; see also Ram Prakash Anand, *Legal Regime of the Sea-Bed and Developing Countries* (Thomson Press (India), 1976); see also Felipe H. Paolillo, "The Institutional Arrangements for the International Sea-Bed and their Impact on the Evolution of International Organisations" *Collected Courses of the Hague Academy of International Law* 188 (1984) 135-338; see also Tullio Treves, *Lo Sfruttamento dei Fondi Marini Internazionali* (Giuffrè, 1982); see also Mohamed Bennoua, "Les droits d'exploitation des ressources minérales des oceans" *Revue Générale de Droit International Public* 84 (1980) 120-143; see also Helmut Tuerk, "The International Seabed Area" in David Joseph Attard, Malgosia Fitzmaurice and Norman A. Martinez Gutierrez , *The IMLI Manual on International Maritime Law* (Oxford University Press, 2014) 276-303; see also Michael W. Lodge, "The Deep Seabed" in Donald Rothwell, Alex Oude Elferink, Karen Scott and Tim Stephens , *The Oxford Handbook of the Law of the Sea* (Oxford University Press, 2015) 226-535.
5. See Introduction.
6. Ibid.
7. See Introduction and Chapters 1, 2 and 3.
8. UNCLOS, Part V, Article 56.
9. Ibid.
10. Ibid.
11. Ibid, Article 58.

12. Ibid, Article 56.
13. Malcolm N. Shaw (n 1) 441.
14. UNCLOS, Part VII, Section 1, Article 87(2).
15. See Chapter 1, Sections 1.3. and 1.4.
16. See Chapter 1, Sections 1.4.1.4.2. and 1.4.1.4.4.
17. See Chapter 1, Section 1.4.1.1.
18. See Chapter 1, Sections 1.3.1., 1.3.1.1. and 1.4.1.3.; see also Chapter 2, Section 2.4.1.
19. See Chapter 2, Section 2.4.
20. UNCLOS, Part V, Article 58.
21. See Chapter 2, Section 2.4.
22. See Chapter 2, Section 2.4.2.
23. See Chapter 2, Section 2.4.
24. See Chapter 2, Section 2.4.
25. See Chapter 2, Section 2.4.1.
26. See Chapter 3, Section 3.6.
27. Mainly the due regard requirement and UNCLOS, Part VII, Section 1, Articles 88 – 115.
28. See Chapter 3, Section 3.5.
29. See Chapter 3, Section 3.5.
30. For example, the requirements of UNCLOS, Part VII, Section 1, Articles 112 – 115.

Bibliography

BOOKS

Abeyratne, Ruwantissa. *Air Navigation Law*. Springer International Publishing, 2012.

Abeyratne, Ruwantissa. *Convention on International Civil Aviation: A Commentary*. Springer International Publishing, 2014.

Allen, Eisner Mark. *Regulatory Politics in Transition*. Johns Hopkins University Press, 2000.

Anand, Ram Prakash. *Legal Regime of the Sea-Bed and Developing Countries*. India: Thomson Press, 1976.

Anand, Ram Prakash. *Origin and Development of the Law of the Sea*. Martinus Nijhoff Publishers, 1982.

Attard, David Joseph. *The Exclusive Economic Zone in International Law*. Clarendon Press, 1987.

Bakardzhieva, Silvina. *The Delimitation of the Contiguous Zone – Implementation of Article 33 of 1983 UNCLOS into Bulgarian Legislation*. Silvina Bakardzhieva, 2015.

Bardonnet, Daniel, Michael Virally, and Guy de Lacharrière. *Le Nouveau Droit International de la Mer*. Editions A. Pedone, 1983.

Birnie, Patricia, Alan Boyle, and Catherine Redgwell, *International Law and the Environment*. Oxford University Press, 2009.

Bowett, Derek. *Law of the Sea*. Manchester University Press, 1967.

Brown, Edward Duncan. *The International Law of the Sea*. Dartmouth, 1994.

Buergenthal, Thomas. *Law Making in the International Civil Aviation Organisation*. University of Virginia Press, 1969.

Buzan, Barry. *Seabed Politics*. Greenwood Publishing Group, 1976.

Cassese, Antonio. *International Law*. Oxford University Press, 2005.

Churchill and Alan Vaughn Lowe, *The Law of the Sea (2 nd Edition)*. Manchester University Press, 1988.

Churchill, Robin, and Alan Vaughn Lowe. *The Law of the Sea (3 rd Edition)*. Manchester University Press, 1999.

Colombos, Constantine John. *The International Law of the Sea*. Longmans, 1967.

Conforti, Benedetto. *Zona Economica Esclusiva*. Giuffrè, 1983.

Cooper, J.C. *The Right to Fly*. New York, 1947.

Crawford, James. *Brownlie's Principles of Public International Law*. Oxford University Press, 2012.

Dahmani, Mohamed. *The Fisheries Regime of the Exclusive Economic Zone*. Martinus Nijhoff Publishers, 1987.

de Ferron, Oliver. *Le droit international de la mer*. Librairie Minard, 1958.

de Yturriaga, José Antonio. *The International Regime of Fisheries: From UNCLOS 1982 to the Presential Sea*. Martinus Nijhoff Publishers, 1997.

Dupuy, Réne Jean, and Daniel Vignes, *A Handbook on the New Law of the Sea: Volume 1*. Martinus Nijhoff Publishers, 1991.

Dupuy, Réne Jean, and Daniel Vignes. *A Handbook on the New Law of the Sea: Volume II*. Martinus Nijhoff Publishers, 1991.

Dupuy, Réne Jean, and Daniel Vignes. *Traité du Nouveau Droit de la Mer*. Economica, 1985.

Erler, Jochen. *Rechtsfragen der ICAO*. Heymann, 1967.

Extavour, Winston Conrad. *The Exclusive Economic Zone: A Study of the Evolution and Progressive Development of the International Law of the Sea*. Sijthoff, 1979.

Fenwick, Judith. *International Profiles on Marine Scientific Research: National Maritime Claims, MSR Jurisdiction, and U.S. Research Clearance Histories for the World's Coastal States*. Woods Hole Oceanographic Institution, 1992.

Gamboa, Melquiades. *A Dictionary of International Law and Diplomacy*. Phoenix Press, 1973.

Gidel, Gilbert. *Le droit international public de la mer*. Mellottee, 1932-1934.

Grotius, Hugo. *The Freedom of the Seas: or, The Right which Belongs to the Dutch to Take Part in the East Indian Trade*. Translated by Ralph Magoffin. Oxford University Press, 1916.

Hailbronner, Kay. *Der Schutz der Luftgrenzen im Frieden*. Heymann, 1972.

Hasselmann, Cord-Georg. *Die Freiheit der Handelsschiffahrt: Eine Analyse der UN-Seerechts-konvention*. N.P. Engel, 1987.

Hayton, Robert. *Jurisdiction of the Littoral State in the "Air Frontier"*. Philippine Society of International Law, 1964.

ICAO, *ICAO: The Story of the International Civil Aviation Organization*. Public Information Office of ICAO, 1969.

Jagota, S.P. *Maritime Boundary*. Martinus Nijhoff Publishers, 1985.

Jennings, Sir Robert, and Sir Arthur Watts. *Oppenheim's International Law*. Oxford University Press, 2008.

Johnson, D.H.N. *Rights in Air Space*. Manchester University Press, 1965.

Karaman, Igor V. *Dispute Resolution in the Law of the Sea*. Martinus Nijhoff Publishers, 2012.

Kolko, Gabriel. *Railroads and Regulation 1877-1916*. Princeton University Press, 1965.

Kwiatkowska, Bárbara. *The 200 [Two Hundred] Mile Exclusive Economic Zone in the New Law of the Sea*. Martinus Nijhoff Publishers, 1989.

Lagoni, Rainer. *Legal Aspects of High Voltage Direct Current (HVDC) Cables*. LIT Verlag, 1999.

Lattion, Renaud. *L'Archipel en Droit International*. Editions Payot, 1984.

Luard, Evan. *The Control of the Sea-Bed: A New International Issue*. Taplinger Publishers, 1974.

Mackenzie, David. *ICAO: A History of the International Civil Aviation Organization*. University of Toronto Press, 2010.

Mangone, Gerard J. *Law for the World Ocean*. Eastern Law House, 1981.

Matte, Nicolas. *Traité de droit aérien-aéronautique: évolution, problèmes spatiaux*. Éditions A. Pedone, 1964.

McDougal, M., and W. Burke, *The Public Order of the Oceans: A Contemporary International Law of the Sea*. Martinus Nijhoff Publishers, 1987.

McDougal, M., H. Lasswell, and I. Vlasic. *Public Order in Space*. Yale University Press, 1964.

Milde, Michael. *International Air Law and ICAO*. Eleven International Publishing, 2008.

Milton, Cooper John. *Pivotal Decades: The United States: 1900-1920*. New York: Norton, 1990.

Moore, John Norton, Myron H. Nordquist, Satya N. Nandan, and Shabtai Rosenne, *United Nations Convention on the Law of the Sea 1982: A Commentary*. Martinus Nijhoff Publishers, 1993.

Mouton, Martinus Willem. *The Continental Shelf*. Martinus Nijhoff Publishers, 1952.

Murchison, J. *The Contiguous Air Space Zone in International Law*. Department of National Defence (Ottawa), 1957.

Nguyen, Quoc Dinh, Patrick Daillier, and Alain Pellet, *Droit International Public*. LGDJ, 2002.
O'Connell, Daniel Patrick. *The International Law of the Sea*. Oxford University Press, 1982-1984.
Orrego Vicuña, Francisco. *The Exclusive Economic Zone, Regime and Legal Nature under International Law*. Cambridge University Press, 1989.
Papadakis, Nikos. *The International Legal Regime of Artificial Islands*. Sijthoff Publications, 1977.
Poúlantzas, Nicholas. *The Right of Hot Pursuit in International Law*. Martinus Nijhoff Publishers, 2002.
Rémond-Gouilloud, Martine. *Droit Maritime*. Editions A. Pedone, 1993.
Roach, J. Ashley, and Robert Smith. *United States Responses to Excessive Maritime Claims*. Springer Netherlands, 1996.
Rothwell, Donald, and Tim Stephens, *The International Law of the Sea*. Hart Publishing Ltd, 2010.
Sauvant, Karl. *The Group of 77: Evolution, Structure, Organization*. Oceana Publications 1981.
Shaw, Malcolm N. *International Law*. Cambridge University Press, 2014.
Shigeru, Oda. *International Law of the Resources of the Sea*. Sijthoff & Noordhoff 1979.
Shigeru, Oda. *The Law of the Sea in Our Time*. Sijthoff, 1977.
Slouka, Zdenek J. *International Custom and the Continental Shelf: A Study in the Dynamics of Customary Rules of International Law*. Martinus Nijhoff Publishers, 2012.
Smith McDougal, Myres, and William Thomas Burke. *The Public Order of the Oceans: A Contemporary International Law of the Sea*. Martinus Nijhoff Publishers, 1987.
Smith, Herbert A. *The Law and Custom of the Sea*. Stevens and Sons Limited, 1959.
Sohn, Louis B., John E. Noyes, Erik Franckx, and Kristen G. Juras. *Cases and Materials on the Law of the Sea*. Martinus Nijhoff, 2014.
Soons, Alfred. *Artificial Islands and Installations in International Law*. Law of the Sea Institute - University of Rhode Island, 1974.
Treves, Tullio. *Lo Sfruttamento dei Fondi Marini Internazionali*. Giuffrè, 1982.
Wang, James. *Handbook on Ocean Politics and Law*. Greenwood Publishing Group, 1992.
Wegelein, Florian H. Th. *Marine Scientific Research: The Operation and Status of Research Vessels and Other Platforms in International Law*. Martinus Nijhoff Publishers, 2005.

CHAPTERS FROM BOOKS

Andreone, Gemma. "The Exclusive Economic Zone" in *The Oxford Handbook of the Law of the Sea* edited by Donald Rothwell, Alex Oude Elferink, Karen Scott, and Tim Stephens. Oxford University Press, 2015.
Attard, David Joseph, and Patricia Mallia. "The High Seas" in *The IMLI Manual on International Maritime Law* edited by David Joseph Attard, Malgosia Fitzmaurice, and Norman A. Martínez Gutiérrez. Oxford University Press, 2014.
Castañeda, Jorge. "Negotiations on the Exclusive Economic Zone at the Third United Nations Conference on the Law of the Sea" in *Essays in International Law in Honour of Judge Manfred Lachs* edited by Jerzy Makarczyk. Martinus Nijhoff Publishers, 1984.
Christol, C.Q. "Unilateral Claims for the Use of Ocean Airspace" in *Law of the Sea: Neglected Issues* edited by J.K. Gamble. University of Hawaii, 1979.
Churchill, Robin. "The 1982 United Nations Convention on the Law of the Sea" in *The Oxford Handbook of the Law of the Sea* edited by Donald Rothwell, Alex Oude Elferink, Karen Scott and Tim Stephens. Oxford University Press, 2015.
Churchill, Robin. "The LOSC Regime for Protection of the Marine Environment – Fit for the Twenty-First Century?" in *Research Handbook on International Marine Environmental Law* edited by Rosemary Rayfuse. Edward Elgar Publishing Ltd, 2015.

Dalal, Hasjim. "The Law of the Sea Convention and Navigational Freedoms" in *Navigational Rights and Freedoms and the Law of the Sea* edited by Donald R. Rothwell, and Sam Bateman. Martinus Nijhoff Publishers, 2000.

De Marffy, Annick. "Marine Scientific Research" in *A Handbook on the New Law of the Sea: Volume 2* edited by Réne Jean Dupuy, and Daniel Vignes. Martinus Nijhoff Publishers, 1991.

Guilfoyle, Douglas. "The High Seas" in *The Oxford Handbook of the Law of the Sea* edited by Donald Rothwell, Alex Oude Elferink, Karen Scott, and Tim Stephens. Oxford University Press, 2015.

Harrison, James. "Actors and Institutions for the Protection of the Marine Environment" in *Research Handbook on International Marine Environmental Law* edited by Rosemary Rayfuse. Edward Elgar Publishing Ltd, 2015.

Heller, P. "Air Space over Extended Jurisdictional Zones" in *Law of the Sea: Neglected Issues* edited by J.K. Gamble. University of Hawaii, 1979.

Klumbyte, Skirmante. "Environment Protection: Pipelines" in *Maritime Safety – Current Problems of Use of the Baltic Sea: Conference in Cooperation with the International Tribunal for the Law of the Sea April 21 st – 23 rd , 2004* edited by Ulrich Karpen. Nomos Publishing House, 2004.

Lagoni, Rainer. "Cables, Submarine" in *Max Planck Encyclopedia of Public International Law* edited by Rudolf Berhnardt. Oxford University Press, 1992.

Lagoni, Rainer. "Pipelines" in *Max Planck Encyclopedia of Public International Law* edited by Rudolf Berhnardt. Oxford University Press, 1992.

Lissitzyn, Oliver. "Freedom of the Air: Scheduled and Non-Scheduled Air Services" in *The Freedom of the Air* edited by McWhinney, and Bradley. McGill University, 1965.

Lodge, Michael W. "The Deep Seabed" in *The Oxford Handbook of the Law of the Sea* edited by Donald Rothwell, Alex Oude Elferink, Karen Scott, and Tim Stephens. Oxford University Press, 2015.

McDorman, Ted L. "The Continental Shelf" in *The Oxford Handbook of the Law of the Sea* edited by Donald Rothwell, Alex Oude Elferink, Karen Scott, and Tim Stephens. Oxford University Press, 2015.

Menash, Thomas. "Submarine Cables and the International Law of the Sea" in *Law of the Sea, From Grotius to the International Tribunal for the Law of the Sea* edited by Lilian del Castillo. Brill Nijhoff, 2015.

O'Connell, D.P. "Innocent Passage of Warships" in *Thesaurus Acroasium of the Institute of Public International Law and International Relations of Thessaloniki: Volume VII.* Thessaloniki Institute of Public International Law and International Relations, 1977.

Oxman, Bernard H. "An Analysis of the Exclusive Economic Zone as formulated in the Informal Composite Negotiating Text" in *Law of the Sea: State Practice in Zones of Special Jurisdiction* edited by Thomas A. Clingan. Honolulu Law of the Sea Institute, 1982.

Pohl, Reynaldo. "The Exclusive Economic Zone in the Light of Negotiations of the Third United Nations Conference on the Law of the Sea" in *The Exclusive Economic Zone: A Latin American Perspective* edited by Francesco Orrego Vicuña. Westview Press, 1984.

Proelss, Alexander. "Pipelines and Protected Sea Areas" in *Shipping, Law and the Marine Environment in the 21 st Century: Emerging Challenges for the Law of the Sea – Legal Implications and Liabilities* edited by Richard Caddell, and Thomas Rhidian. Lawtext Publishing Ltd, 2013.

Roberts, Walter. "The State of the Art in Weather Modification" in *Weather Modification and the Law* edited by H.J. Taubenfeld. Oceana Publications, 1968.

Scerni, Mario. "La Zone Économique Exclusive: Son Importance, sa Nature Juridique et les Problèmes Principaux Relatifs" in *Thesaurus Acroasium of the Institute of Public International Law and International Relations of Thessaloniki: Volume VII.* Thessaloniki Institute of Public International Law and International Relations, 1977.

Schreiber, Alfonso. "The Exclusive Economic Zone: its Legal Nature and the Problem of Military Uses" in *The Exclusive Economic Zone: a Latin American Perspective* edited by Francesco Orrego Vicuña. Westview Press, 1984.

Stephens, Tim, and Donald Rothwell. "Marine Scientific Research" in *The Oxford Handbook of the Law of the Sea* edited by Donald Rothwell, Alex Oude Elferink, Karen Scott, and Tim Stephens. Oxford University Press, 2015.

Symonides, Janusz. "Problems and Controversies Concerning Freedom of Navigation in the Arctic" in *Law of the Sea, From Grotius to the International Tribunal for the Law of the Sea* edited by Lilian del Castillo. Brill Nijhoff, 2015.

Tanaka, Yoshifumi. "Principles of International Marine Environmental Law" in *Research Handbook on International Marine Environmental Law* edited by Rosemary Rayfuse. Edward Elgar Publishing Ltd, 2015.

Treves, Tullio. "Historical Development of the Law of the Sea." In *The Oxford Handbook of the Law of the Sea* edited by Donald Rothwell, Alex Oude Elferink, Karen Scott, and Tim Stephens. Oxford University Press, 2015.

Tuerk, Helmut. "The International Seabed Area" in *The IMLI Manual on International Maritime Law* edited by David Joseph Attard, Malgosia Fitzmaurice, and Norman A. Martínez Gutiérrez. Oxford University Press, 2014.

Wolfrum, Rüdiger. "The Freedom of Navigation: Modern Challenges" in *Law of the Sea, From Grotius to the International Tribunal for the Law of the Sea* edited by Lilian del Castillo. Brill Nijhoff, 2015.

PERIODICALS/JOURNALS

Abeyratne, Ruwantissa. "In Search of Theoretical Justification for Air Defense Identification Zones." *Journal of Transportation Security* 5, (2012): 87.

Al Mour, Awadh Mohamed. "The Legal Status of the Exclusive Economic Zone." *Revue Egyptienne de Droit International* 33, (1977): 35.

Allen, Craig. "Doctrine of Hot Pursuit: A Functional Interpretation Adaptable to Emerging Maritime Law Enforcement Technologies and Practices." *Ocean Development and International Law* 20, (1989): 309.

Allott, Philip. "Mare Nostrum: A New International Law of the Sea." *American Journal of International Law* 86, (1992): 764.

Armas Barea, Calixto, and Frida Pfirter de Armas. "Consideraciones Sobre la Naturaleza Jurídica la Zona Económica Exclusiva." *Anuario Argentino de Derecho Internactional* (1983): 37.

Bateman, Sam. "Hydrographic Surveying in the EEZ: Differences and Overlaps with Marine Scientific Research." *Marine Policy* (2005): 163.

Becker, Michael A. "The Shifting Public Order of the Oceans: Freedom of Navigation and the Interdiction at Sea." *Harvard International Law Journal* 46, (2005): 131.

Bennoua, Mohamed. "Les droits d'exploitation des ressources minérales des oceans." *Revue Générale de Droit International Public* 84, (1980): 120.

Birnie, Patricia. "Law of the Sea and Ocean Resources: Implications for Marine Scientific Research." *International Journal of Marine and Coastal Law* (1995): 229.

Boyle, Alan. "Further Development of the 1982 Convention on the Law of the Sea: Mechanisms for Change." *International and Comparative Law Quarterly* (2005): 563.

Brown, E.D. "The Exclusive Economic Zone: Criteria and Machinery for the Resolution of International Conflicts between Different Users of the EEZ." *Maritime Policy and Management* 4, (1977): 325.

Burke, William. "Exclusive Fisheries Zones and Freedom of Navigation." *San Diego Law Review* 20, (1983): 595.

Caflisch, Lucius and Jacques Piccard. "The Legal Regime of Marine Scientific Research and the Third United Nations Conference on the Law of the Sea." *Zeitschrift für ausländisches öffentliches Recht* 1978: 848.

Charney, Jonathan I. "The Exclusive Economic Zone and Public International Law." *Ocean Development and International Law* 15, (1985): 233.

Christol, C.Q. "Aircraft and the International Legal and Institutional Aspects of the Stratospheric Ozone Problem." *Annals of Air and Space Law* (1976): 3.

Clingan, Thomas A. "Freedom of Navigation in a Post-UNCLOS III Environment." *Law and Contemporary Problems* 46, (1983): 107.

Clingan, Thomas. "Emerging Law of the Sea: The Economic Zone Dilemma." *San Diego Law Review* 14, (1977): 530.

Copes, Parzival. "The Impact of UNCLOS III on Management of the World's Fisheries." *Marine Policy* 5, (1981): 217.

Crowley, John. "International Law and Coastal State Control over the Laying of Submarine Pipelines on the Continental Shelf." *Nordic Journal of International Law* (1987): 40.

Dale, Andrew. "Archipelagos and the Law of the Sea." *Marine Policy* 2, (1978): 45.

Davenport, Tara. "Submarine Communications Cables and Law of the Sea: Problems in Law and Practice." *Ocean Development and International Law* (2012): 201.

de Muralt, R.W.G. "The Military Aspects of the U.N. Law of the Sea Convention." *Netherlands International Law Review* 32, (1985): 78.

Degan, V. D. "Internal Waters." *Netherlands Yearbook of International Law* 17, (1986): 3.

Dulaney, Michael, and Robert Merrick. "Legal Issues in Cross-Border Oil and Gas Pipelines." *Journal of Energy and Natural Resources Law* (2005): 247.

Dutton, Peter. "Caelium Liberum: Air Defence Identification Zones Outside Sovereign Airspace." *American Journal of International Law* 103, (2009): 691.

Fitzmaurice, Sir Gerald. "Some Results of the Geneva Conference on the Law of the Sea." *International and Comparative Law Quarterly* 8, (1959): 73.

Flenn, Percy Thomas. "Origins of the Theory of Territorial Waters." *American Journal of International Law* 20, (1926): 465.

Francioni, Francesco. "Peacetime Use of Force, Military Activities, and the New Law of the Sea." *Cornell International Law Journal* 18, (1985): 203.

Franklin, Mark. "Sovereignty and Functional Airspace Blocks." *Air Space Law* 32, (2007): 425.

Georgiades, E. "Du Nationalisme Aerien a 1'Internationalisme Spatial ou le Mythe de la Souverainete Aerienne." *Revue Française de Droit Aérien Spatial* (1962): 129.

Gidel, Gilbert. "La Mer Territoriale et la Zone Contiguë." *Collected Courses of the Hague Academy of International Law* 48, (1934): 241.

Gündling, Lothar. "Die Exclusive Wirtschaftszone." *Zeitschrift für Ausländisches Öffentliches Recht* 38, (1978): 616.

Gutteridge, J.A.C. "The 1958 Convention on the Continental Shelf." *British Yearbook of International Law* 35, (1959): 102.

Hailbronner, Kay. "Freedom of the Air and the Convention on the Law of the Sea." *The American Journal of International Law* 77, (1983): 490.

Head, Ivan L. "ADIZ, International Law and Contiguous Airspace." *Alberta Law Review* (1964): 182.

Hollick, Ann L. "The Origins of 200 Mile Offshore Zones." *American Journal of International Law* 71, (1977): 494.

Hurst, Sir Cecil. "Whose is the Bed of the Sea?" *British Yearbook of International Law* 4, (1923-1924): 34.

Jaenicke, Günther. "Die Dritte Seerechtskonferenz der Vereinten Nationen." *Zeitschrift für Ausländisches Recht und Völkerrecht* 38, (1978): 438.

Kiss, A.Ch. "La Pollution du milieu marin." *Zeitschrift für ausländisches öffentliches Recht* (1978): 902.

Knight, Gary. "International Legal Aspects of Deep Draft Harbour Facilities." *Journal of Maritime Law and Commerce* 4, (1973): 367.

Larson, David. "Security Issues and the Law of the Sea: A General Framework." *Ocean Development and International Law* 15, (1985): 99.

Lawrence, William H. "Superports, Airports and Other Fixed Installations on the High Seas." *Journal of Maritime Law and Commerce* 6, (1975): 575.

Lewis, Alexander, and Robert Hodgson. "The Impact of the 200-Mile Economic Zone on the Law of the Sea." *San Diego Law Review* 12, (1975): 569.

Lott, Alexander. "Marine Environmental Protection and Transboundary Pipeline Projects: A Case Study of the Nord Stream Pipeline." *Utrecht Journal of International and European Law* (2011): 51.

Magdelénat, Jean-Louis. "Les Implications de la Nouvelle Convention sur le Droit de la Mere en Droit Aérien." *Annuaire de Droit Maritime et Aérien* 8, (1985): 323.

McDougal, Myres S. and Schlei, Norbert A. 'The Hydrogen Bomb Tests in Perspective: Lawful Measures for Security' [1955] The Yale Law Journal 648

Mensah, Thomas. "The Dispute Settlement Regime of the 1982 United Nations Convention on the Law of the Sea." *Max Planck Yearbook of United Nations Law* (1998): 307.

Milde, Michael. "United Nations Convention on the Law of the Sea – Possible Implications for International Air Law." *Annals of Air and Space Law* 8, (1983): 167.

Moore, John Norton. "The Regime of Straits and the Third United Nations Conference on the Law of the Sea." *American Journal of International Law* 74, (1980): 77.

Morris, Michael. "Military Aspects of the Exclusive Economic Zone." *Ocean Yearbook* 3, (1982): 320.

Mudrić, Mišo. "Rights of States Regarding Underwater Cables and Pipelines." *Australian Resources and Energy Law Journal* (2010): 235.

Münch, Fritz. "Les Iles Artificielles et les Installations en Mer." *Zeitschrift für Ausländisches Öffentliches Recht* 38, (1978): 933.

Oda, Shigeru. "The Concept of the Contiguous Zone." *International and Comparative Law Quarterly* 11, (1962): 131.

Oelofsen, P.D. "Some Observations on the Concept of the Exclusive Economic Zone." *South African Yearbook of International Law* 1, (1975): 46.

Oxman, Bernard H. "The Third United Nations Conference on the Law of the Sea: the 1976 New York Session." *American Journal of International Law* 72, (1977): 247.

Paolillo, Felipe H. "The Institutional Arrangements for the International Sea-Bed and their Impact on the Evolution of International Organisations." *Collected Courses of the Hague Academy of International Law* 188, (1984): 135.

Petras, Christopher. "The Law of Air Mobility: the International Legal Principles behind the U.S. Mobility Air Forces' Mission." *Air Force Law Review* 66 (2010): 1.

Poulantzas, Nickolaos. "The Right of Hot Pursuit Especially Under the Geneva Convention on the High Seas." *Revue Hellénique de Droit International* 14, (1961): 198.

Pradelle, Paul. "Les frontières de l'air." *Recueil Des Cours* 86, (1954): 117.

Puri, Rama. "Evolution of the Concept of the Exclusive Economic Zone in UNCLOS III: India's Contribution." *Journal of the Indian Law Institute* 22 (1980): 497.

Rauch, Elmar. "Military Uses of the Oceans." *German Yearbook of International Law* 28, (1985): 229.

Richardson, Elliot. "Law of the Sea: Navigation and Other Traditional Security Considerations." *San Diego Law Review* 19, (1982): 553.

Robertson, Horace B. "Navigation in the Exclusive Economic Zone." *Virginia Journal of International Law* 24, (1984): 865.

Roggenkamp, Martha M. "Petroleum Pipelines in the North Sea: Questions of Jurisdiction and Practical Solutions." *Journal of Energy and Natural Resources Law* (1998): 92.

Schwenk, Walter. "Die Anwendung luftrechtlicher Vorschriften bei Flügen von und nach Schiffen und Bohrinseln." *Zeitschrift für Luft- und Weltraumrecht* (1976): 234.

Thomas, A.R., and James C. Duncan. "Annotated Supplement to The Commander's Handbook on the Law of Naval Operations." *International Law Studies* 73, (1999): 99.

Treves, Tullio. "Codification du Droit International et Pratique des Etats dans le Droit de le Mer." *Collected Courses of the Hague Academy of International Law* 223, (1990): 9.

Truver, Scott. "The Law of the Sea and the Military Use of the Oceans in 2010." *Louisiana Law Review* 45, (1984): 1221.

Vinogradov, Sergei. "Challenges of Nord Stream: Streamlining International Legal Frameworks and Regimes for Submarine Pipelines." *German Yearbook of International Law* (2009): 241.

Walker, Craig. "Jurisdictional Problems Created by Artificial Islands." *San Diego Law Review* 10, (1973): 638.

Whiteman, Marjorie M. "Conference on the Law of the Sea: Convention on the Continental Shelf." *American Journal of International Law* 52, (1958): 629.

Williams, Andrew. "The Interception of Civil Aircraft over the High Seas in the Global War on Terror." *Air Force Law Review* 73, (2007): 73.

Wolfrum, Rüdiger. "Der Schutz der Meeresforschung in Völkerrecht." *German Year Book of International Law* (1976): 99.

Young, Richard. "The Legal Regime of the Deep Sea Floor." *American Journal of International Law* 62, (1968): 641.

WEBSITES

Centre for Tankship Excellence website: http://www.c4tx.org/ctx/job/cdb/precis.php5?key=19780316_001

Group of 77 website: http://www.g77.org/doc/

ICAO website: http://www.icao.int/about-icao/Pages/default.aspx

IMO International Maritime Law Institute website: http://www.imli.org/about-us/imli-library

International Cable Protection Committee website: www.iscpc.org

Legal Information Institute (Cornell University Law School) website: https://www.law.cornell.edu/wex/customary_international_law

National Oceanic and Atmospheric Administration (U.S. Department of Commerce) website: http://www.noaa.gov/ocean.html

Nations Encyclopaedia website: http://www.nationsencyclopedia.com/United-Nations-Related-Agencies/The-International-Civil-Aviation-Organization-ICAO-ACTIVITIES.html

United Nations (Frequently Asked Questions) website: http://www.un.org/Depts/los/LEGISLATIONANDTREATIES/frequently_asked_questions.htm

CONFERENCE PAPERS

Robert Beckman, and Tara Davenport, "The EEZ Regime: Reflections after 30 Years" [2012] LOSI Conference Papers

Robert Beckman, "Submarine Cables – A Critically Important but Neglected Area of the Law of the Sea" (7TH International Conference on Legal Regimes of Sea, Air, Space and Antarctica, New Delhi, January 2010)

REPORTS

Report of the International Law Commission covering the work of its eighth session, article 27 (ILC, 1956)

Hendrick Acker and Stephen Hodgson, *Legal Aspects of Maritime Spatial Planning* (Fish/2006/09)

ARTICLES

Jeremy Page, "The A to Z on China's Air Defense Identification Zone" *The Wall Street Journal* (27 November 2013)

Marjo Vierros, Anne McDonald, and Salvatore Arico, "Governance of marine areas beyond national jurisdictions" *UNU Rio+20 Series 1* (2012)

WORKING PAPERS

Yoshinobu Takei, "Law and Policy for International Submarine Cables in the Asia-Pacific Region" (2011) Asian Society of International Law Working Paper 2010/13
UN Doc. A/CONF.62/C.2/L.68 (1974) by El Salvador

ICPC RECOMMENDATIONS

ICPC Recommendation 2 (2008)
ICPC Recommendation 3 (2008)
ICPC Recommendation 6 (2008)

FOREIGN LEGISLATION

Hepburn Act of 1906 (United States)
Exclusive Economic Zone Act (Malaysia)
The Territorial Waters, Continental Shelf, Exclusive Economic Zone and Other Maritime Zones Act (India)
Exclusive Economic Zone and Continental Shelf Act (China)
Regulations on Management of Laying Submarine Cables and Pipelines (China)
Territorial Waters and Maritime Zones Act (Pakistan)

PROPOSALS

UN Doc. A/CONF.13/C.2/L.3 (1958) by Mexico
UN Doc. A/CONF.13/C.5/L.15 (1958) by Switzerland
UN Doc. A/CONF.13/C.2/L.68 (1958) by the United Kingdom
UN Doc. A/A.138/SC.II/L.45 (1973) by China
UN Doc. A/AC.138/SC.II/L.21 by Columbia, Mexico and Venezuela
UN Doc. A/CONF.13/C.2/L.30 by Czechoslovakia, Poland, the Soviet Union and Yugoslavia
UN Doc. A/CONF.13/C.2/L.71 by India
Seabed Committee 1973 Session Proposal A/AC.138/SC.II/L.34 by China

OTHER SOURCES

GATT documentation at the CIESIN Thematic Guide
Rüdiger Wolfrum, "Freedom of Navigation: New Challenges" (International Tribunal for the Law of the Sea)
De Jure Praedae of 1609
Informal Composite Negotiating Text (Office of Law of the Sea Negotiations, Department of State 1977)